Football Classified

An Anthology of Soccer

EDITED BY

Willis Hall & Michael Parkinson

FOREWORD BY

H.R.H. the Duke of Edinburgh, K.G., K.T.

William Luscombe Publisher Limited
(in association with Mitchell Beazley)

First published in Great Britain by
William Luscombe Publisher Limited
Artists House
14 Manette Street
London W1V 5LB

ISBN 0 86002 062 2

Filmset in Monophoto Baskerville by
Servis Filmsetting Limited, Manchester

Printed in Great Britain by
Tinling (1973) Limited, Prescot, Lancs

The authors' and illustrator's royalties
from the sale of this book have been entirely
donated to the Goaldiggers' Trust

Contents

Foreword

by
H.R.H. the Duke of Edinburgh, K.G., K.T., Goaldiggers' Coach

This is the second football anthology to be compiled as a donation to the Goaldiggers, an organisation that exists solely to help provide, or improve, pitches or just play areas where children and young people can kick a ball about in safety.

It may sound simple, but it is probably one of the most important social contributions it is possible to make.

As space for play and casual games, particularly in towns, becomes scarcer and more expensive, the natural inclination of children and young people to play and take part in games becomes more and more frustrated. The need for grass or hard surfaced pitches in urban areas – and in villages too sometimes – is urgent. So the Goaldiggers can truthfully claim to be concerned with the grass – or asphalt – roots of soccer, but to do anything about it they need money.

Willis Hall and Michael Parkinson, two of the founder members of the Goaldiggers Club, have again put an interesting book together, with generous contributions from many busy people and I hope this year's publication will be as great a success as the one before.

Philip

Introduction

There was once an editor who invented a trap for budding journalists. "What do you want to be, young man?" he would say. Inevitably, the answer would be "A sports writer or a film critic, Sir" providing him with his cute retort: "Sports writers are drunken oafs, film critics are dreamers I have no use for either on my paper."

We suffered the routine, which is how we became film buffs and sports writers. The combination of beer swilling, raffish dreamer proved irresistible. We are not saying that every writer contained in the following pages lives up to that description, but we are suggesting that everyone who has ever tried the craft of sports reporting has felt from time to time the chill contempt of his fellow professionals.

In the social hierarchy of journalism the leader writers, those people who tell us today what we knew the day before, are the aristocrats. Then in ascending order of merit, come financial journalists, lobby correspondents, political journalists, political cartoonists, industrial correspondents and the like. So it continues until you reach the bargain basement where you will find the football writer sandwiched in between William Hickey and Rip Kirby, making up the bottom three and in constant danger of being relegated, which is why so many journalists will write about football and sometimes do silly things like offering to eat their brown bowler hats if Leeds don't win the League. It is not that they are exhibitionists, simply lost souls crying for recognition in the wilderness. Nor is their status any more elevated once they leave the office. They are asked to work in conditions any sewage rat would consider offensive. On the whole, press boxes give every indication of being built by the same joker who designed the Black Hole of Calcutta, and the hospitality of the majority of football clubs is conspicuous by its absence. They are required to glean their copy from directors, who, in the main, find it difficult to count to five with their gloves on. Moreover, they are expected to promote as Gods, athletes whose intelligence often rises no higher than the third lacehole on their left boot.

That they manage the task at all argues well for their physical resilience and intellectual adaptability. In the final analysis it can be argued that no-one forces them to do the job and that it is far preferable to digging coal for a living. And that of course is true. The simple fact is that soccer writers, like lion tamers and steeple-jacks, are in love with their job. They accept the axiom that it is not necessary to have a slate loose to report soccer, but if you have it actually helps. In the following pages you will read some of the best work of these practitioners of an extraordinary craft. You will also read articles and stories about soccer by people who make their livings in different fields. They share one thing in common with those people who sweat it out in the press box – they love the game and they don't care who knows it.

The Editors

Bruddersford United A.F.C.

J. B. Priestley

Something very queer is happening in that narrow thoroughfare to the west of the town. It is called Manchester Road because it actually leads you to that city, though in order to get there you will have to climb to the windy roof of England and spend an hour or two with the curlews. What is so queer about it now is that the road itself cannot be seen at all. A grey-green tide flows sluggishly down its length. It is a tide of cloth caps.

These caps have just left the ground of the Bruddersford United Association Football Club. Thirty-five thousand men and boys have just seen what most of them call "t'United" play Bolton Wanderers. Many of them should never have been there at all.

It would not be difficult to prove by statistics and those mournful little budgets (How A Man May Live – or rather, avoid death – on 35 Shillings a Week) that seem to attract some minds, that these fellows could not afford the entrance fee. When some mills are only working half the week and others not at all, a shilling is a respectable sum of money. It would puzzle an economist to discover where all these shillings came from.

But if he lived in Bruddersford, though he might still wonder where they came from, he would certainly understand why they were produced. To say that these men paid their shillings to watch twenty-two hirelings kick a ball is merely to say that a violin is wood and catgut, that *Hamlet* is so much paper and ink.

For a shilling the Bruddersford United A.F.C. offered you Conflict and Art; it turned you into a critic, happy in your judgement of fine points, ready in a second to estimate the worth of a well-judged pass, a run down the touch-line, a lightning shot, a clearance kick by back or goalkeeper; it turned you into a partisan, holding your breath when the ball came sailing into your own goalmouth, ecstatic when your forwards raced away towards the opposite goal, elated, downcast, bitter, triumphant by turns at the fortunes of your side, watching a ball shape *Iliads* and *Odysseys* for you. . . .

And what is more, it turned you into a member of a new

13

community, all brothers together for an hour and a half, for not only had you escaped from the clanking machinery of this lesser life, from work, wages, rent, doles, sick pay, insurance-cards, nagging wives, ailing children, bad bosses, idle workmen, but you had escaped with most of your mates and your neighbours, with half the town, and there you were, cheering together, thumping one another on the shoulders, swopping judgements like lords of the earth, having pushed your way through a turnstile into another and altogether more splendid kind of life, hurtling with Conflict and yet passionate and beautiful in its Art.

Moreover, it offered you more than a shilling's worth of material for talk during the rest of the week. A man who had missed the last home match of "t'United" had to enter social life on tiptoe in Bruddersford.

As he moved slowly down Manchester Road, the press of fellow spectators still thick about him, Mr Oakroyd found himself brooding over the hollow vanities of this life. He felt unusually depressed. His physical condition may have had something to do with it, for he was hot, dusty and tired; there had been a full morning's hard

"The last derby game was so good that I wasn't even noticed . . . Have a heart, lads."

work for him at the mill; he had hurried through his dinner; walked to the ground, and he had been on his feet ever since. Manchester Road after a match had never seemed so narrow and airless; a chap could hardly breathe in such a crowd of folk.

And what a match it had been! For once he was sorry he had come. No score at all. Not a single goal on either side. Even a goal against the United would have been something, would have wakened them up a bit.

The first half had been nothing but exasperation, with the United all round the Wanderers' goal but never able to score; centres clean flung away, open goals missed, crazy football. The second half had not even been that, nothing but aimless kicking about on both sides, a kids' game.

During the time that it took him to progress 300 yards down the crowded road, Mr Oakroyd gave himself up to these bitter reflections. A little farther along, where there was more room, he was able to give them tongue, for he jostled an acquaintance who turned round and recognised him.

"Na Jess!" said the acquaintance, taking an imitation calabash pipe out of his mouth and then winking mysteriously.

"Na Jim!" returned Mr Oakroyd. This "Na" which must once have been "Now", is the recognised salutation in Bruddersford, and the fact that it sounds more like a word of caution than a word of greeting is by no means surprising. You have to be careful in Bruddersford.

"Well," said Jim, falling into step, "what did you think on 'em?"

"Think on 'em!" Mr Oakroyd made a number of noises with his tongue to show what he thought of them.

"Ah thowt t'United'a'made rings rahnd'em," Jim remarked.

"So they owt to 'a' done," said Mr Oakroyd, with great bitterness. "And so they would 'a' done if they'd nobbut tried a bit. I've seen 'em better ner this when they've lost. They were better ner this when they lost to Newcastle t'other week, better bi far."

"Ay, a seet better," said the other. "Did you ivver see sick a match! Ah'd as soon go and see 'tschooil lads at it. A shilling fair thrawn away, ah call it." And for a moment he brooded over his lost shilling. Then, suddenly changing his tone and becoming very aggressive, he went on: "Yon new centre-forward they've getton – MacDermott, or whativver he calls hissen – he'll nivver be owt, nivver. He were like a great lass on t'job. And what did they pay for him? Wer it two thahsand pahnd?"

"Ay." Mr Oakroyd made this monosyllable very expressive.

"Two thahsand pahnd. That's abaht a hundred for ivvery goal

he missed today. Watson were worth twenty on 'im – ah liked that lad, and if they'd let him alone, he'd'a' done summat for 'em. And then they go and get this MacDermott and pay two thahsand pahnd for him to kick t'ball ower top!'' Jim lit his yellow monster of a pipe and puffed away with an air of great satisfaction. He had obviously found a topic that would carry him comfortably through that evening, in the taproom of *The Hare and Hounds*, the next morning, in the East Bruddersford Working Men's Club and possibly Sunday, Monday and Tuesday nights.

Mr Oakroyd walked on in silence, quickening his pace now that the crowd was not so thick and there was room to move. At the corner of Manchester Road and Shuttle Street, both men halted, for here their paths diverged.

"Ah'll tell tha what it is, Jess," said his companion, pointing the stem of his pipe and becoming broader in his Yorkshire as he grew more philosophical. "If t'United had less brass to lake wi', they'd lake better fooitball." His eyes searched the past for a moment, looking for the team that had less money and had played better football. "Tha can remember when t'club had nivver set eyes on two thahsand pahnds, when t'job lot wor not worth two thahsand pahnds, pavilion an' all, and what sort of fooitball did they lake then? We knaw, don't we? They could gi' thee summat worth watching then. Nah, it's all nowt, like t'ale an' baccy they ask so mich for – money fair thrawn away, ah calls it."

"Well, we mun 'a' wer teas and get ower it. Behave thi-sen, Jess!" And he turned away, for that final word of caution was only one of Bruddersford's familiar good-byes.

"Ay," replied Mr Oakroyd dispiritedly. "So long, Jim!"

From *The Good Companions*, 1928

Sweden v. Brazil, 1958

Geoffrey Green

The summit meeting of football is over. Brazil are the new world champions and a long awaited ambition has at last come true for them. In the first final between the New and the Old worlds it was they, the lordly representatives of the New, who brought a lustre, a magical quality that dazzled Sweden. It was a climax that had a 52,000 crowd holding its breath in wonder from the start to finish here in the Rasunda Stadium – from the moment when Sweden took a swift lead through Liedholm, only to find themselves finally bewildered by a brand of football craft beyond the understanding of many.

Here were dark, expressive sportsmen of a distant continent. When the moment of triumph was finally sounded by the whistle, in an excited, demonstrative and kindly way they broke into triumphal circuit of the soft battlefield scarred by rain, brandishing above their heads a huge Swedish flag – a gesture of appreciation for their reception. The stadium stood to them as if it were the host nation herself who had won, and at the end the King of Sweden himself posed for photographs with the victors while many of them were openly overcome by their achievement.

After 28 years of effort Brazil were the World Champions. To the Briton, perhaps, such scenes might seem far-fetched. But warmth, and an undisguised emotionalism, gushes out of the Brazilians. So it was as Mr Drewry, president of FIFA, presented the gold statuette to Bellini, Brazil's captain, that he said in echoing terms: "Here indeed was a match to remember, a clean, sporting struggle between two great teams." Every word was true. None could disagree with that, for here indeed *was* a match to remember. Perhaps one of the finest ever played in history came four years ago in Switzerland when Hungary overcame Uruguay in the semi-final round. This, perhaps, lacked the fire of that other occasion, but for sheer skill it was little behind. The cycles of the game, unfortunately, seldom coincide. If only it were possible to put Puskas and his Hungarians of 1954 on the field with the Brazil of today. But that must be something for one's dreams.

17

The bones of today's performance were these: at the fifth minute Liedholm, completing a slick penetrating move with Bergmark, Borjesson and Simonsson, beat two men on a sixpenny piece and shot home low to put Sweden one up. On a slithery green pitch, as glistening as the rooftops of Stockholm after a night and morning of rain, it now looked as if the favourites were in for trouble. The Swedes had got the first blow and the South Americans, so rumour has it, are unhappy in the wet.

But rumour was not put to flight summarily as Vava, at centre-forward after all, with goals in the ninth minute and then again at the half-hour, put Brazil 2–1 ahead by the interval. After that Pele and Zagallo made it 4–1, and though Simonsson brought Sweden back to 4–2, the swarthy Pele, leaping like a black panther, headed Brazil to 5–2 as the last seconds of a breathtaking exposition ran out. Brazil, in fact, proved that they could play in the wet.

Thus Sweden, a fine side by any standards, were finally run into the ground by a brand of footballing dexterity that knew no bounds. Strongly and bravely as the Swedish defenders faced the surging tide – Gustavsson, Bergmark and Borjesson in particular – they were at times left spinning like tops. Gren, especially, Simonsson and Liedholm too worked heroically in attack, thread-ing many a subtle central move. But where they were stifled was out on the flanks and that, if nothing else mattered, finally settled their fate. Hamrin and Skoglund, their match-winners in the past, were now blanketed by the majestic covering of D. Santos and N. Santos at full-back and Sweden's sharpest fangs were drawn.

Not so Brazil. Didi, floating about mysteriously in midfield, was also the master link, the dynamo setting his attack into swift motion; and, besides Didi, with Vava and Pele a piercing double central thrust, they had the one man above all others to turn pumpkins into coaches and mice into men – Garrincha, at outside-right. Rightly has he been called the Matthews of the New World. His methods are the same: the suggestion of the inward pass, the body-swerve, the flick past the defender's left side, and the glide to freedom at an unbelievable acceleration. Poor Axbom stuck to him the best he could, but time after time he was left as lonely as a mountain wind. Garrincha, in fact, and the subtle use made of him by Didi in a swiftly changing thread of infiltration, was beyond control and that was that. There lay the most sensitive nerve-centre of the whole battle and so Brazil stretched out and grasped their ambition.

This Brazilian side was greater than their combination of eight years ago because of its defence; and it was in another world to the side that lost 2–4 to England at Wembley in 1955. England alone held them here in the World Cup. It seems incredible to think of it now, but over the last fortnight the Brazilians have been growing in stature and today they reached their zenith. They showed football as a different conception; they killed the white skidding ball from all angles as if it was a lump of cotton wool. From Gylmar in goal, the giant Bellini at centre-half, right through the team, they were fused in swift, intimate thought and execution at changing tempos. They combined the theatrical with the practical and Sweden too often were left chasing shadows.

It was in fact a performance of superlatives and Brazil came to life that moment at the ninth minute when Garrincha receiving from Didi, left Axbom stranded, swept into the by-line for Vava to flash in his diagonal cross. That was 1–1 and a moment later Pele nearly uprooted the Swedish post with a left foot shot from 20 yards. But there was no holding Garrincha and again at the half-hour it was the old echo – Pele, Didi, Garrincha, the flick, the by-line, the diagonal cross, and Vava striking again at close range. Ten minutes after the change of ends, Pele with sleight of foot jugglery, flicked up a cross from Zagallo, balanced the ball on his instep, chipped it over Gustavsson and leapt round the centre-half to volley home. Who can live with this sort of stuff?

That was 3–1 to Brazil and the signal for individual exhibition in all corners of the field. Then it was 4–1 as Zagallo, cutting in on a rebound punished a mistake by Bergmark. Liedholm, with a long through pass, put Simonsson beautifully in for 4–2; and there might have been a penalty at each end as Sweden rallied fiercely and momentarily. But all hope was gone, and a swift header by Pele from Zagallo's cross wrote the last word.

SWEDEN: Svensson; Bergmark, Axbom; Borjesson, Gustvasson, Parling; Hamrin, Gren, Simonsson, Liedholm, Skoglund.

BRAZIL: Gylmar; D. Santos, N. Santos; Zito, Bellini, Orlando; Garrincha, Didi, Vava, Pele, Zagallo.

From *The Times*, 1958

19

The Manager

Ian Wooldridge

Brash, belligerent, coarse, honest, treacherous, crude, intelligent, likeable, frank, sensitive, blunt, perceptive, liberal, fascist, brainless and quite impossible were just a few of the adjectives applied during the sporting year of 1973 to a football manager named Brian Clough.

The very volume of the descriptions testifies to the fact that it was Clough's year. The wildly contradictory reactions he roused imply that few know the real character of the man. It is a brave or foolish reporter who attempts to define so here, as they say, goes:

Watching him on television is like staring into a volcano. You see fire and colour and turmoil. The manner is histrionic, the voice harsh and rasping, the opinions scabrous.

Studying him from close quarters you see a different man. There are questions, too. "God," he cries, in anguish. "Where is this Good Life that people talk about? We haven't found it yet, kid."

Materially, he has made it. He has contempt for money and spends it hugely. I estimate his gross income last year more than £40,000.

But in a moment of confession, behind closed doors when the audience was small, he conceded: "I've made this pressure for myself. You see, I can't afford the comfort of being a failure.

"I shout my opinions. I yell my contempt. I mean every word of it. But when you talk like that you are a target. I've got to be a winner or they'll cut me to pieces."

There are those who see that as the condition that would make him an ideal successor to Sir Alf Ramsey as England manager. But what kind of a man would England be getting?

A man, I fancy, who is striving for inner peace but realises he is now too committed to the contest.

He was holding court in a group of eight the other night when it emerged that one of the company was a former priest. Clough pounced: "Why did you pack it in?" he shouted.

The man said quietly: "I didn't pack it in completely. I'm still a practising Christian."

"I'd like an hour with you," said Clough. "I'd like *six* hours with you. I'd like to say I had beliefs like that. Something solid."

Clough has a depressive streak, too. "Success?" he says. "Tell me that date when my obituary is going to appear and I'll tell you whether I've been a success or not. If I get to 60 I shall have done pretty well."

Perhaps it is this macabre thought that drives him to live a 40-hour day, 10-day week. Every moment is filled with noise and tumult, and Clough is compelled to dominate every scene. He cuts the vital engagements fine and is late for others.

His only concession to his health is that he stopped smoking completely $3\frac{1}{2}$ years ago. The manner in which he did it is revealing:

"I was smoking 40 cigarettes a day. The chairman of Derby County gave me two boxes of *Romeo y Julieta* cigars and said they'd be better for me. I smoked the whole lot in three days. I sent out for another two boxes. The bill was £25. I stopped there and then."

Today he drinks a good deal of champagne. Whether he pays for it or someone else is quite immaterial. He is enormously generous and quite savage about people who are not.

At the time of the cigar incident his relationship with the Derby chairman, Sam Longson, was so close that Longson once suggested that he would like to investigate legal methods that would permit him to adopt Clough. "I'd like you to take over my business one day," he told Clough.

Nothing came of it. Now neither man can scarcely spare a good word for the other.

Clough's bullying is not confined to his players. He can be ruthless with bad service in hotels. He fills a room with electrifying urgency and booms his disapproval if he is kept waiting. He always picks on the boss, never the waiter.

Returning once from a TV performance in London, he took two friends into an hotel for dinner. In the rush of the day, they had neither cheque-books nor money. They raised 78p between them.

Clough, taken aback that the manager did not recognise him, instructed him to ring one of his hotel directors to confirm that his credit was good. Clough then looked across the restaurant at a young man who appeared to be hitch-hiking to nowhere. "And put that chap's meal on my bill as well," he told the manager.

He can be venomously critical. He can be as generous with praise as he is with his money.

He instantly concedes his debt to Peter Taylor, the assistant manager who has become inseparable in every venture in Soccer:

"I am not equipped to manage successfully without him," he

says. "I am the shop front. He is the goods in the back.

"Peter's strength is that he has the ability to see things 24 hours before I do. I like time if the decision has to be right. In assessing a player, for example. I like three weeks. Peter often has to do it in 90 minutes."

His doubts concern the motives that drive him on and where, if anywhere, they are rushing him headlong.

"We drive the best cars, we live in the best hotels, we are the product of the best that a thousand years of civilisation can give us," he said.

"But we are strained and we are tense and we never stop. It isn't my definition of the Good Life, but I don't know what is."

Brian Clough, of course, will never be England manager. They couldn't pay him enough.

From the Daily Mail, 1973

Spotted

Peter Terson

The play is set in a factory yard where workmen and apprentices are whiling away their lunch hour.

WAGS: I knew he was there, this scout. I knew he was there.

DICKER: How did you know him?

WAGS: I kept my ear to the ground. Funny thing was, he wasn't there to watch me.

DICKER: Go on, who was he there to watch?

WAGS: The opposing centre-half.

(*Enter* JIMMY)

JIMMY: Hear you got spotted, Wags.

WAGS: Yeah, did Jimmy. They were there watching the opposing centre-half, really.

JIMMY: But they spotted you?

WAGS: I'll tell you some time, Jimmy.

JIMMY: Right then, mate. That's a date, feller.

(*Enter* SPOW *and* GARRETT)

SPOW: Hear you got spotted, Wags.

WAGS: Don't let it turn your head then, Spow. You old fellers shouldn't get ideas.

SPOW: You got spotted like a dalmatian gets spotted, from its arse to its tip.

GARRET: These young 'uns are always being bloody spotted for something or the other, pop singing, or football or that. Anything but bloody work.

JIMMY: What do you put in your Thermos this weather, Garretty?

GARRET: Lemonade, you daft bastard.

JIMMY: Then you could keep it in a bottle, and save your Thermos for the winter. You'd save a fortune in refills.

SPOW: Your mother would save a fortune if she had your head refilled.

(*Enter* HARRY *and* BAGLEY)

BAGLEY: Hear you were spotted then, Wagsy.

WAGS: Yeah. Scouts from Birmingham City and Manchester United.

BAGLEY: I don't believe that.

WAGS: Believe what you like, but it's true. Scouts. They came to watch the opposing centre-half, not me.

BAGLEY: Hadn't they heard of our Wagsy?

WAGS: No. They don't watch works teams.

BAGLEY: Why's that then?

WAGS: They think you're all tied up with your apprenticeship.

HARRY: I like that. Tied, what do they think we are? Prisoners?

BAGLEY: I feel like it in this heat. I had a look at the flesh under all this the other day. Repulsive. Like melted cheese. That French stuff.

DICKER: Wensleydale.

BAGLEY: That's the stuff. With bits of tomato in, that's my skin. You'll be all right, you'll be under bloody sun-ray treatment.

WAGS: We get all that.

HARRY: How did you shine out then, Wags?

BAGLEY: Natural talent.

WAGS: I knew they were looking at their centre-half like, and he was looking good against our centre-forward. I was playing on the wing, old-fashioned! Our team has the tactics of bloody Julius Caesar. I said to the captain, that big centre lathe turner from B shed, "I want to play the four–two–four" and he said, "You'll play on the wing like and get knotted," so I thought, "This is no good to me. They're stifling my talent. I'm a natural link man." But there's no link man in our team.

BAGLEY: No idea of modern football.

WAGS: So I went and linked up. I kept pulling the ball out of the defence, dribbling midfield, like United, and luring the big daft centre-half.

BAGLEY: Big, was he?

DICKER: Wags made him look like a carthorse. I was there.

WAGS: He was good in the air.

DICKER: So Wags kept it low. He just brought it down, and took it in low.

WAGS: The centre-half came over to me at half time. . . .

BAGLEY: What a sportsman.

WAGS: And he said, "Leave me alone or I'll screw you in the second half."

DICKER: He didn't leave him alone, though. He took it to him all the time.

WAGS: The scouts both came up to me, and said they'd see my father about offering me terms.

DICKER: Come on, Wags, try a shot.

(*They canter off*)

24

BAGLEY: Offering terms? I hadn't thought of this before. We're prisoners. We're offered terms to get out. Wags is escaping.

From *The Apprentices*, 1967

Three Fives

Julie Welch

As centre-halves go, Jim Holton is less buxom than some and considerably more implacable than others – a bony, booted, gangling threat who patrols in defence with the soft tread of an elephant's rumba. As footballers in general go, Holton is not without his basic skills, and he positions well, heads panoramically, and likes to bring to a dangerous situation the self-belief of a ruthless disinfectant.

He came from Shrewsbury Town at the beginning of 1973. Then he was 21, so keen to go to Manchester United that he brought along six Biros in case Docherty's ran out when the moment came to sign. "They were so glamorous, the first team in England that you thought of," he says, and adds regretfully: "It used to be such a great team, and there's no way the men in the club now can replace it."

Most people, knowing Holton only from the grubby proximity of the stands and terraces, and the sweet confines of the armchair and the telly, will have a fixed image of that large young man, uncoiffed, gap-toothed, urgently thumping a ball out of play or goggling disappointedly at his beaten goalkeeper. He looks as charismatic as barbed wire.

It may surprise the same people to hear that Holton in his public moments is precisely the sort of mannerly, presentable lad every mother would like to see calling for her daughter – if he hadn't, that is, been married for nearly two years.

There is about Holton a self-assurance and maturity unusual in a footballer of few years, few clubs, and no social notoriety. While not exactly expecting him to bite anyone's legs, his approach should have at least brought on an apprehensive feeling in the tibias – in fact, like that other well-loved guard dog in a shirt, Norman Hunter, his off-field presence is absolutely disarming.

Like most players who have a 5 tattooed on their jerseys, and probably their psyches as well, he has few illusions about the nature of his game.

"I imagine myself as a centre-forward, scoring goals all the time, but it'll never happen. A lot of skill is a bonus for a centre-half. I'm there to get the ball away from the danger area, and if I started trying to be skilful, it would take something away from the game. People criticise United, saying we're all hard – but I'm really the only one in the team who's a physical player.

"I try to use my assets to the best of my ability. I see a bloke and I want to get the ball. That's all I feel. I don't like hurting players, and you must emphasise that because a lot of people think I do it intentionally. But when I tackle a bloke I want him to know he's been tackled.

"I think I'm valuable to the team because I keep on trying. I like to think I encourage the others: I'm one of those people who keeps on encouraging."

The fact that Manchester United – hallowed past, desperate present and all – are in imminent danger of sliding down the relegation snake, seems not to depress Holton one bit. With a bit more luck than they've been having, when they've had a run of three or four wins. . . .

And if he is believed, which he deserves to be, the atmosphere in the team now is so good that if they were on top, it cannot be imagined what they would be like, short of laughing maniacally and frothing at the mouth.

He attributes the good atmosphere to Docherty. The influence of that manager – friendly, good-humoured and nowadays probably a smiling worry-guts – is strong on Holton, who talks admiringly of the way he motivates his players.

"I have great respect for him, and I hope he feels the same respect for me. And from him up to the chairman, they're all fantastic. They go out of their way to make you happy. At a lot of clubs, these people are untouchable, they won't say a word to you. But not here.

"The present situation must be very hard for a team like Manchester United – they've been bred on success for so long. Now we're down, everybody wants a kick. But if we do get relegated – which as I told you, we won't – it's the First Division that will suffer."

A lot of hard men share Holton's brand of club loyalty. A player of destructive intent and blunted skills gives little joy to all but the most partisan, and receives criticism and ridicule from outsiders. His club, on the other hand, endorses him and protects him.

Thus this player will put up a barrier against the outside and turn his ambitions inwards to become a "good club man" – only the club understands his worth, so how can he help identifying with it?

This is putting things at their most simple – Holton is not now only valuable to Manchester United, but also to the Scottish team.

Perhaps the aggrieved hoots of opposing supporters in Germany will be drowned out by the frenzied fierce bias that only the Scots reserve for their particular heroes.

Peter Corrigan

Stationed solidly at the centre of Birmingham City's defence, Roger Hynd has a method of withstanding the pressures of the First Division relegation battle. It involves a careful avoidance of the subject when he isn't playing, and a studied collision with opponents when he is.

If the approach appears basic, the philosophy behind it has a surprising depth. Besides being a large and powerful Scot, Hynd is an intelligent and well-educated man. One should not express amazement at that, but when a player's style is more like the slamming of a dungeon door than the opening of a book of wisdom, the inclination is not to take a thick notebook to the interview.

Hynd would not welcome such a train of thought, for he makes a virtue of his simplistic approach and tends to champion all those who make up for their deficiencies with added commitment and dedication.

"To say there is no room for my type of player, or any type of player, is wrong. Football thrives on the differences of its participants. Complete professionalism is the only thing they need to share. Every man is God when he has the ball.

"I am not paid for being pretty; I am paid for being effective. And if a situation calls for a neatly placed ball into the back row of the stand, that is where it is going. I've no dribbling skills; I am just a basic player whose strengths are in my running and my . . . . . (he thought carefully for the word) stoppability. No one yet has been able to make me think I'm not good enough, just as no one can make me think that Birmingham are not good enough to stay in the First Division – and even more, become one of the top teams."

We had been talking just before the news that Freddie Goodwin, the Birmingham manager, had broken all sorts of records in the transfer of his brilliant centre-forward, Bob Latchford, to Everton in exchange for Howard Kendall, full-back Archie Styles and some loose change to the value of £80,000.

It was a drastic move, and although Hynd admires the positive, he was as stunned as anyone in and around St Andrews.

But the real issue was soon back in control: "You tend to accept

*"We don't have to stick rigidly to the itinerary, lad. Constable says
we can report to the station first if we like."*

facts in football. Problems are set to make you think, not to make
you worry. Was it Oscar Wilde who said that? Anyhow, the manager is thinking like a professional and acting like one. His is the
responsibility of blending the team. All we have to do as individuals
is to make sure our mental attitude stays right."

I had hoped to hear from him something more of the strain of
being involved in a relegation zone, which, because for the first
time three teams must go down, has an added frenzy. But he declined
to discuss it, just as he had deleted the First Division table from
his list of required reading and shies from being interested in the
activities of Birmingham's rivals.

"Pressure is a disease, and you catch it by fretting about things
outside your control. And once you catch it you twitch and panic
and act out of character. I don't even look at the fixture lists. I
got up on Sunday and wondered who we would be playing this
week. It was Wolves.

"So I think about Wolves, and on Friday night I will go to bed
early and get out my notes about Wolves. Some of them are my
own jottings from the past, others are revealing clippings from
newspapers. And I will read about how one of their forwards
sometimes drops back so the midfield man can hit the runner

through. Then I will read about Dougan and about Wagstaffe, and when I am fully concentrated, I will sleep like a baby. It's just like revising the night before an exam."

Hynd has known a number of exams. He was a part-timer with Glasgow Rangers while he went through school and college to graduate as a teacher of physical education. There is no need to point out the irony in the fact that Jim Holton, his counterpart at Manchester United, was a pupil of his at Lesmahagow Higher Grade school near Lanark. And while we are name-dropping, it might as well be mentioned that Bill Shankly is his uncle.

"Yes," says Hynd, "Bill is my mother's brother: Uncle Bill, or, rather, Target Bill. I have to have targets, whether in football or in finance or home: I need to have something to aim at. One of them is to do better in football than Uncle Bill. All right, so it is a tall order . . . but perhaps the taller the better.

"It's the way I compensate myself. I wasn't going to be a brilliant player, so I've made myself a bloody good club man. I'm 32 years old, and I look around at the competition and think perhaps I have four years left and then I'll be a bloody good manager."

He acknowledges that he might have been a better player had he been brought to England as a 16-year-old and subjected to the professional approach he admires in English football. But he did not become a full-time professional with Rangers until he was 23, and after two years went back to teaching and part-time football. He was 27 when Crystal Palace wanted to buy him, and he took a deal of convincing before returning to the game full-time.

"I was intrigued by the family atmosphere at Palace. Then, when Birmingham came for me four years ago, I was similarly impressed with Freddie Goodwin and with the city of Birmingham. The support here is tremendous, and they deserve the standard of football we will eventually bring them. They made me feel like a king when I came here, and I do as much as I can in the community – they pay my wages, and I can do more than just kicking a ball about for them.

"There are a lot of players with degrees, but I wonder if they use the benefits of their education within the club and within the community. Well, that's their business. Whether it is helping kids or charities or making presentations or speeches, I love it. This is a great city, and I wish I had been here 10 years and not four. I regret that I will probably never teach again. But there is the compensation of helping kids in soccer – I love working with them and I wish every club would concentrate on looking after their welfare and preparation for the game.

"I sometimes wonder how they are affected by all the clogging that goes on. I will never deliberately clog anyone – look at my record; it's good. I believe in contact, though. A fair tackle, body to body, doesn't really hurt because there are no sharp, protruding edges when you tackle someone fairly."

Perhaps there is the consolation for some of Roger Hynd's opponents in the vital matches ahead: no protruding edges, just an uncomfortable feeling that they have stood in the way of someone on a very important errand.

Alan Road

"You can tell some of those centre-forwards that I'm not the big, bad man that I'm cracked up to be." It was Duncan Forbes's parting shot as he dropped me at Norwich Station and drove off to visit a team mate in hospital for a cartilage operation.

Big he is not. At 31, Norwich City's Scottish centre-half still tips the scales short of 12 stone and he is under 6 ft. Bad he would not dispute, although there is no denying that this former Edinburgh wages clerk is currently calculating the wages of sin with some anxiety.

After missing the opening games of the season under suspension he is now only two points from another break, thanks to five bookings in five months. If one more referee dips his hand into his baggy pants for the black book, Norwich will be deprived of Forbes's service at a crucial stage in their fight to avoid relegation.

"I just go out there and try to forget it," he says, but clearly it adds substantially to the pressures of being at the centre of a defence where every goal conceded can represent a deadly decimal in the final reckoning.

Manager John Bond, too, knows what a blow another booking could be to his team. "As captain, his greatest quality is his influence on the other players," he says. "Even if we are three down he still goes for everything."

Pointing to his five times broken nose and his missing teeth, Forbes claims he is, in fact more sinned against than sinning. At Highbury last season he went into the Arsenal penalty area for a corner-kick and, as the ball floated over, a knee in his back broke a rib, which punctured a lung. Forbes claims he harbours no grudges and even speaks appreciatively of the way Arsenal players visited him in hospital. Centre-forwards reading with relief of his indisposition were sadly premature, for within a month Forbes was back.

31

When pressed, however, he will admit that whenever Norwich find themselves opposed to a side which operates with a pair of strikers, he finds himself marking the hard man. "When we play Leeds, with Jones and Clarke, I mark Jones. When we play Wolves, with Dougan and Richards, I mark Dougan." Of course, with the tight-marking that is such a feature of modern play, twin centre-halves going up for set pieces draw twin strikers back with them and cause congestion in penalty areas. "There's often a wall of bodies across the goalmouth and the referee often has his work cut out to see what is going on," says Forbes.

One of the things going on in Norwich's penalty area is a battle of wills between Forbes and his opposite number. "My main job," he says, moving beer-mats along the bar to demonstrate tactical moves, "is to inflict myself on the attacker. From the very start I've got to assert my authority on him." If the outcome of his attentions is that the opponent is unable to play his normal game and spectators are consequently derived of their entertainment, that's too bad.

Looking back over his career, punctuated by more finger waggings from referees than he would care to count, Forbes is touchingly proud of the fact that he has never been sent off. "I would never go over the top and I don't think I have ever injured anyone seriously." If he thought he had, he would be very upset. "I'm not a bad chap really."

Not that you can afford to be too nice in football. "You can't have players thinking you've gone soft." Perish the thought.

From *The Observer*, 1974

Editorial Note : When the article containing the profiles of these three centre-halves was first published, their respective teams were labouring at the foot of the First Division. At the end of the '73/'74 season, of the three, only Birmingham survived the drop, Norwich City and Manchester United being relegated along with Southampton.

The Dying Footballer

Brian Glanville

"That's right!" he said, in a loud, brash Geordie voice. "That's right! A big fellow with a bullet head! I heard you! I heard you in the cinema!"

Sitting there, he seemed to rise out of the bed as sudden and irrelevant as a Triton; the rough, grey jersey, the square, red, wind-whipped face, belonged not to a sanatorium but to ships, fields, stadiums.

"I didn't know. . . ." I said, and stopped, the attack too strong and unexpected. I had probably made the remark, but then I had never seen him, had only heard about him, and the image I had formed was precisely that: a big fellow with a bullet head. Looking at him now, I could see that he was big indeed, but that the head was uncompromisingly square. In the bed beside him, Williams, a small grey-headed Welshman, smiled a secret and diverted smile, and reached for the sputum mug on his pedestal.

"I was right in front of you," Marshall said, "*Now* then!" His expression was one of challenge, as though he dared me to deny it, his voice the same brass monotone, and it was several moments before I realised that he was not annoyed, that this vehemence might simply be his way of statement. But embarrassment had paralysed me; I mumbled quickly the message I'd been given for them, and I left the room.

A few days later, I had cause to visit them again, this time with a trolley of library books. All those patients who were out of bed had jobs to do, and this was one of mine. Their room was at the very end of the long, dim, ground-floor corridor and when I reached it, I hesitated before knocking on the door.

"Come in!" The voice was not that of a sick man; again I wondered what had brought Marshall here.

"What, fetched us some books?" he asked, without reproach. "Let's see 'em, let's 'ave a look at what you've got."

"Here you are, then," I said, annoyed that he should take it for granted.

"Daphne Du Maurier? That's no bloody good to me! Haven't

33

you got anything new? Something by Mickey Spillane? Something with a bit of meat in it?"

"No."

"Then I'll get 'em from home," he said, "I will," and leaned back against his throne of pillows.

I had planned to talk to him about his club – the one he managed, and the others he had played for – but at this I muttered, "All right, then" and wheeled the trolley from the room.

"Here, come back!" he called, "come back!" but I took no notice.

A week later Dr Cowley said to me, his lean, brown face alive with a joke he would not share, his smile private and condescending, "You can talk about football all day long, now. Mutual therapy. I'm moving you in with a professional."

"Billy Marshall?" I said. "But can't I stay in this room?"

"We need it," he said. "There's a much more serious case than you coming. We're only keeping you because we want to teach you some discipline, anyway."

"But isn't there someone else?"

"*No* one else," he said, his anger rising quickly, as it always did when he was opposed. He was at the door now, disdaining to look at me. "No one else. If you don't want *that* bed, you can go home."

The next afternoon, I moved in with Billy Marshall.

"Hallo, lad," he said. "I'm glad to see you here. I'd rather have you than that other fellow; coughing and spitting all the time, hawking into his cup. It was filthy; filthy."

I nodded morosely at him, and looked out of the window. Beyond the putting lawn, where a group of patients was engaged in desultory play, a rank of pine trees grew like watch-towers, their pale, thick bark like the scales of immense crocodiles. Through them, again, one saw the Norfolk fields, pale and unemphatic, gently rising into a grey distance.

"How old are you, lad?" Marshall asked, behind me. "Nineteen? That's a bit bloody young to be in a sanatorium. They tell me you're an Arsenal fan, as well."

"I am," I said, turning round slowly.

"You're a bit of a fan of something else, too. Eh? *I've* seen you from here, from the window. *I've* seen you with that girl, that what's it."

"Have you?"

"Ah, and you needn't try that," he cried, with pointing finger, "making out you don't know what I'm on about. *I've* seen; I'm not bloody blind."

"I'm sure you're not."

34

I undressed in silence, got into bed, and opened a book without another word.

"Here, have you seen this?" he said. There was a rustle, something landed on my bed, and, looking up, I saw that a green newspaper, a Football Final, was lying there, irresistible. I thanked him.

"Two goals up," he said, "and let in three in the last 20 minutes. I know 'em. There's no one there to talk to the buggers. They let up, it went to their head."

The paper came from the Yorkshire coast town whose Third Division club he managed. There was a kick by kick match report, spreading over two pages – "Town were moving well now and a sizzling 20 yard drive by star forward Jimmy Wall smashed against United's upright; United's goal was bearing a charmed life" a honeycomb of local league results, a page of minute, compulsive team analysis.

"You were unlucky to go down last season," I said.

"Unlucky? We weren't unlucky, we were swindled down, it was a bloody scandal. What about the team that stayed up, eh? What about the last match of the season, the one they won away from home, when their centre-half went round the other dressing-room with a bundle of five-pound notes? You can't prove it, you can't get at them, but when I see bloody Stewart, I'll tell him, he'll hear something. I've never had time for that bugger."

"What, the manager of Rovers?"

"If I had my way, he'd be manager of bloody Dartmoor, I've told him so, I've known him 20 years. He's a rogue, that's what he is, a rogue. I knew him when we were both running clubs in the Lancashire Combination; he was with Runcorn, I was player-manager of Rossendale. We went there for a match one day and the gateman said, 'Where's your card? You can't come in without your card, Mr Stewart's orders,' and I said, 'Bugger Stewart, I'm the manager. You go and tell Stewart I'm here.'

"So he came out and I said to him, 'What's all this about?' and he said, 'You know you're meant to have your registration card, you know it's a League rule,' and I said, 'Bugger that,' and I pushed him in the chest, I pushed him all the way down the bloody corridor."

I could imagine him doing it. The first giant tactlessness, the sudden gesture, and now this anecdote, revealed him as a force of nature, devoid alike of ruth and malice, so that the common courtesies were not disregarded, but simply unknown. Thus, our days together were pregnant with surprise; my own at sudden monstrous violations of tact, and his surprise at my resentment.

35

Then there would be temporary silences, each of us prisoned in our own astonishment, till the silence would change in quality, from hostility to armistice, and a gesture – usually his – would bring peace again.

He had two visitors during our first week together. One was his wife; she was his own age, a blonde matron-figure, fitting shapelessly into shapeless clothes, all smiles and mild, clucking amazement. Her cheeks were heavy with rouge. She, too, was from the North East, but she had its soft, persuasive accent, where his was vehement and hard; they talked together with a quick, low intimacy. Now and then, there were moments of apparent tension. I could not hear what they said, but she seemed to be pressing him, and his voice would rise, with a note of obstinacy. For all his present illness, I had an impression that she had somehow abdicated from life, while he had not.

There was a son, born late in the marriage, 10 years old, but he hadn't come; when Marshall spoke about him it was with a certain reluctant pride, as though he were aware of an Achilles' heel. "Kicks well, he does that; left foot or right."

The second visitor was less expected. She came one afternoon when Marshall was asleep, her auburn head peering round the door a moment, uncertain. Then, opening the door a little farther, she tip-toed into the room, a tall, handsome, large-breasted woman, perhaps in her early thirties. "Billy?" she whispered, and again, a little louder, "Billy?"

His head turned on the pillow, he gave a snort, then sat up very quickly, looking at her. "I'll be buggered. I was asleep."

"I wrote you I was coming." She spoke with a Yorkshire accent.

"I know you did, I know." He gestured at me and said, "This is Brian."

"The other one's gone, then."

"Well, tell me," he said. "Come on, tell me." He took her hands and she sat down by him, on the bed. I picked up a book and turned my back on them, in deference to their intimacy, but they spoke very little, only a murmur now and then, and once their silence grew so protracted and intense I imagined they must be kissing.

When she'd gone, he did not talk about her, and it was three weeks before she came again. I wondered if his wife knew, and had a notion that she did; at times I'd sensed in her attitude a lurking reproach, and in his an evasive guilt.

It wasn't long before he, too, was allowed to get up and begin the series of graduated walks across the bland, flat country; to the white gate, the stone bridge, the village, and at length, beyond it, to the windmill, the church, the railway station, the sea shore. Marshall would put on corduroy trousers, his jersey, a tweed cap; sometimes he would carry a stick. He walked with a slow, heavy stride, saying, "Go on, lad, go on, I can't keep up with you, I wish I had your wind."

There was something about him that was vaguely obsolete, and at the same time, reminiscent. Later, I identified this feeling with an old, forgotten photograph – of footballers abroad on a Continental tour, between the wars; flat caps, baggy suits off the peg, an impression of stiffness and unease, the Depression invisible in the background. It was from these years that Marshall had emerged, as player, first, then manager, one of the "old school", cut off from the new wave of blue blazers, muted accents, quiet conformity – "If you eat peas with a knife, now, they won't put you in the England team." He'd been born in one of those little Northumberland mining villages where footballers sprouted like dragons' teeth, had turned professional – "Newcastle bloody daft and I signed for Sunderland" – played five times for England, became a player-manager, then a manager.

While we walked, he would talk about all this; of goals, games, players, great victories, unjust defeats. Through his whole narrative ran a thread of rough acceptance; you were hard and football was hard, and football was hard because life was hard. "I had bloody Dougald with me, three year before the war; there was still no one could play like him when he wanted; he could still have played for Scotland, only they'd never have him again after what had gone on, drunk every bloody night. I took a risk, see; I gambled on him. One morning they had a fight in the dressing-room, him and that bloody Irishman, Donnon. Donnon gave him a black eye, and by the time I'd heard of it and went down there, they'd gone, they'd gone to bloody Dougald's house for dinner! I wanted to suspend the two of them, but the Board wouldn't have it, so I took 'em both down to Fulham for the Saturday and Dougald broke his bloody leg."

He wouldn't be in the sanatorium long – he was sure of that, and so was I. "Lie on the bed, do this, do the bloody other. I said to the sister the first day I was here, 'Look, bugger off,' I said, 'you can ask me,' I said, 'you can't bloody *tell* me, nobody can.' Then *he* comes round the other day, the little one with the big nose, the patients' committee, he says, 'You're up now, you're delivering papers down this corridor.' 'I'm bloody not,' I said, 'not if you put it like that. If you ask me properly, I'll do it; willingly. Started off selling papers in Newcastle, I don't mind going back to it now.' "

Even Dr Cowley was wary of him, playing him carefully and respectfully, like some angler who has inadvertently hooked a shark. "All right today, Marshall? Temperature still on-side?"

And Marshall, looking at him, cautious and impassive, "Ay, all right, doctor. Just tell me the day I can go, that's all."

He had a posse of friends, Northerners, like himself, who would emerge from their nooks and crannies on the hillside – from lofts, from chalets on the hillside – to surround him for a steady grumble, for mutual rough consolation: Jack Grace, wuth his bald head and his insinuating chuckle, little Dave Oliphant, with his auburn moustache, his bent shoulders and his grinding omniscience; Ernie Jacks, who was 60, a Yorkshire leprechaun, living in a private and inaccessible world. "The doctors? Booger the doctors!"

"Ay, but you can't bugger tham all, Ernie," said Marshall.

"*He* can!" chuckled Grace. "Can't you, Ernie?"

They were all polite to me, but I wasn't one of them, hadn't the common experience, the years, the vernacular, the responses and reactions. I was cautious with them when we were together, glad they seldom joined us on our walks, some because they were still largely bedridden, others because we went too fast and too far.

"Mad boogers the pair of 'em," Ernie would say.

Sometimes as we walked, Marshall would ask, "What am I doing here?" echoing the question that was in my own mind. What, indeed? "Never a *day's* ill-health; never a day. Two cartilages out and a broken leg; that's the only time I've ever been in a hospital."

"Then how did you get *this*?"

"How? I don't know, buggered if I do. I asked the doctor at home; he said, overwork. Overwork? I said. I've worked like this for 20 years. He said, ay, but you're not young anymore. Well, I'm not old, I said; I'm not so bloody old."

I could see, at the moment, that in his own eyes he would always be young, and it was this that made his wife seem older than he – this that enabled him to keep the auburn girl, with her big breasts and her nascent sensuality. "I'll be out in a month," he said. "Two months and I'll be running the bloody club again. I told 'em."

In the meantime he went to the clinic once a week, "to get pumped up" – or for his "A.P. refill", as the other patients called it. But Marshall never acquired the sanatorium vocabulary; "thora", "A.Ps.", "P.Ps.", "refills", "strep", "P.A.S.". It was as though by rejecting it, he somehow denied the reality of his illness, his involvement with the rest of us.

38

The next time his wife came, she brought their son. He was a lively, fair-haired child, with sturdy, plump, pink knees; he climbed on the bed in his excitement while behind him his mother uselessly exclaimed: "David, don't crawl on him! Get off the bed, will you?"

"He's all right," Marshall said, grabbing the boy and rolling him on his back. She watched them without more protest, almost with resentment, as if she knew that she would always be excluded.

"I were in the school team, Dad! I played and I scored three!"

"You're coming on, you're coming on."

Marshall was beginning, now, to agitate. When Dr Cowley came round in the evenings, he would say, "How about a date, then, doctor? My temperature's still down. I'm gaining weight. I feel well." And Dr Cowley would reply, "Not yet, not yet, it won't be long."

"Ay, but how long? Two weeks? A month?"

"Softly, softly catchee monkey," Dr Cowley said, and disappeared with his crooked, self-conscious smile.

"I'll give him monkey. We'll be up for bloody re-election by the time I get out."

For his team wasn't doing well, in that Northern Section where the names fell like dry ice on the heart; Barrow, Rochdale, Tranmere, Accrington. It was Accrington, indeed, who beat them 6–0, after they had failed to win one of their last four home games. "I wrote to them. I told them they'd get a hiding there, if the wing-halves carried the ball. Both of them go up together, the others break away and they've got the whole park in front of them. And they send missionaries to Africa . . ."

Autumn turned to winter. It snowed, and the snow dropped slowly from the pines and lay thick upon the hill, with its pink-roofed chalets. The little red flags of the putting lawn rose here and there above the snow carpet like buoys in a white sea. We would spend hours together in the recreation room, playing a game called Disc-Bat Cricket; a game at which I always won.

"Makes his own bloody rules!" he would shout, calling on all present to bear witness. "Two fielders inside the circle; *he* can do it: *you* can't!" And sometimes I would lose my temper, shouting back, forgetting that to him a shout meant as little as a shrug, and must never be taken at its face value.

The draw for the F.A. Cup was made; by chance the Rovers, "Bloody Stewart's" club, had been drawn to play nearby, at Norwich. "I'll be there if it does for me," said Marshall. "I'll be there if I go in a bloody ambulance."

The auburn-haired woman came again, and this time, I was able to go out of the room and leave them. An hour later, returning to go back to bed, I found she was still there. Marshall had already got into bed, and she sat there as she had before, her hand in his. "I'll go out," she said, but before she could move there was an eager pattering in the corridor, the door was hurled open, and Marshall's little boy appeared.

"Hallo," said Marshall, looking up. "Clash of fixtures here."

The women, confronted, gave each other one pregnant glance – shock and detestation on the one side, guilt, resentment and a covert defiance on the other, then there was silence. The three of them might have been frozen by a Gorgon's head, with only the little boy bewildered and alive.

"Well," the younger woman said at last, "I'll be going then." She climbed off the bed, pulled her dress down with a crisp defiance, said flatly, "Get better soon, then, Bill," exchanged tight-lipped goodbyes with Mrs Marshall, and left the room. As the door began to close, Marshall found his voice, roaring after her, "Look after yourself, now."

"She's always done that," his wife said, with low intensity, while the little boy cried, "Who's that, Dad? Who's that lady? Why did she go?"

"Just a friend, that's all," he said. "She was passing through. She was going to Norwich."

Lying on the next bed, I feigned that I could neither see nor hear, sharing their agony, wondering how long his wife would stay, what they could find to say while she did. But it was the little boy who saved them, busy with his questions, so that Marshall could talk to him while his wife, still sitting there, withdrew, till such time as she could decently leave him. I sensed in her hostile farewell to me that I was included in her indictment, that simply through being there, when she was not, I had somehow conspired to betray her.

"These things happen," Marshall said, when she had gone, "you can't help them," but within half an hour, resignation gave way to good cheer, and he was telling me about Fred Westgarth, the manager of Hartlepools. "He's a rough diamond, Fred, a rough diamond. I rang him up once about fixtures. He said, 'When shall we play?' I said, 'New Year's Day.' He said, 'New Year's Dee? New Year's Dee? When's that?' "

As the day of the Cup-tie approached, he talked increasingly of "Bloody Stewart".

"*He'll* be surprised. He'll never reckon on seeing *me* there. And

I'll tell him in front of the lot of them. I will."

We stood by the mill pond, beneath the silent windmill; three swans floated motionless, haughty and serene. "*I'll* wake 'em up," said Marshall, "sitting there like they own the place." He beat his stick hard and fast against the boards skirting the pool, and at once the three swans turned and made towards him in a menacing glide, quick and effortless, the mean little heads extended at the end of their long, white, powerful necks. "I'll show 'em. Break their bloody necks, I will." For the moment, they were Stewart-surrogates.

The first swan hissed and struck, and I backed uneasily away, but Marshall merely stepped aside, and nudged it with the flat of his stick. "I should leave them," I said, "they'll be out of the water." But he took no notice, defiant, just as in past days he must have defied a packed defence.

"*Go* on! Get off, you buggers!"

With a flap of wings, a second swan climbed out of the pond, but again Marshall side-stepped, pushing it away, until the three of them confronted him, hissing and dripping, he motionless, the stick extended. The tableau lasted for perhaps 30 seconds, then all at once dissolved as the swans, one by one, turned and scuttled back into the pond. "There you are," said Marshall, "I told you so. Stand up to them. That's all you've got to do." And somehow the whole incident seemed characteristic of him, not only for his defiance, but for the aggression which had made defiance necessary.

At first, Dr Cowley did not want to let him go to Norwich; to deter him he assumed his "ruthless" tone. "If you really want to get pleurisy, you can go, so long as you don't expect me to look after you when you've got it."

"I don't expect anything, doctor; I never have, never in me life."

And so we went, the two of us together, went by taxi, with two tickets for the directors' box. "He'll get a shock," Marshall kept saying, as we sped over the snow-powdered roads, past the dappled fields, past the villages, with their neat Tudor churches. We ate at a Norwich restaurant, full of rowdy, red-faced men, wearing the green and gold favours of the City, shouting in the broad quick Norfolk accents, "Up the Canaries!" and from time to time bursting into song:

> "*On* the ball, the City!
> Never mind the *dan*-ger!"

Beyond the ugly railway siding, down the mud track, past the bleak canal, the Stadium was a vacuum pump, sucking the city dry. The air was crisp and very cold, and there was movement everywhere; the fans were bowling along together, side by side, as though to a family occasion.

"*I'll* give him bloody relegation," Marshall said. A commissionaire showed us to the Board Room, afume with whisky, beer and cigarette smoke, but the sanatorium had conditioned us, and we sheered away, making for the open air. Beneath the directors' box, the stadium surged with colour and expectancy. The Norwich mascot was a tall, gaunt man with an umbrella, dressed up to look like a canary, with a great artificial beak, a mass of green and yellow "feathers", and a bell which – together with the nose – completed a sinister resemblance to The Bellman in the Duchess of Malfi.

When Stewart climbed into the directors' box, Marshall greeted him with, "Now then, Tommy!" and Stewart recoiled, as far as his short, plump figure would allow him; a little, round-faced man with silver hair and quick, pale, cunning eyes. "Never thought *you'd* be here, Billy."

"Ay, I bet you never did!"

"Heard you'd been ill," Stewart said. It was one of those voices which had begun in the North, to be planed and deracinated by years in the South. "Getting better, are you?"

"None the bloody better for seeing you," said Marshall, while the directors' box filled up, each newcomer pausing to observe the cameo, astonished, interested or wary. "Just tell me how you won that last match, eh? Just tell me how you kept out of the Second Division. That's all I've come to ask you."

"I don't know what you mean, Billy," Stewart said, looking away from him."

"That last match at Frinton Park. *You* know."

"Fair and square, Bill," said Stewart, "we won it fair and square. I'm surprised at you, complaining."

"Bought it fair and square, you mean!" cried Marshall, while a hubbub of voices rose to drown his own, and Stewart cried, "You be careful, Bill! I can have you into court for that, it's slander!"

"Have me, then!" Marshall shouted. "Have me if you bloody dare! And have your bloody centre-half, as well! The one with the fivers!"

Forgetting, once again, the special nature of his violence, I wondered whether he was going to hit Stewart, and then, what I would do if he did. For he could not be allowed to do anything so self-destructive, so reckless of the sanatorium code of careful preservation. "Billy," I cried, taking his arm, but he paid no notice

42

to me. Stewart was very still and quiet, like some hunted animal which seeks escape through stealth and self-effacement, his eyes turned slyly away. Below the directors' box, spectators were standing up and looking round and indeed, all over the grand-stand, clumps of people were rising to their feet, heads were turning curiously towards us. How the scene would have ended I don't know, but it was destroyed in a moment by a sudden, surging roar, a roar taken up all over the stadium – "Up the Canaries!" as the Norwich team, in green and gold, ran on to the field.

"*I* told the bugger," Marshall said, and sat down, evidently satisfied.

At half-time, in the Board Room, people were chary of us, but Marshall was heartily at ease, greeting those he knew, sweeping them into conversation despite themselves. In any case, one saw that he was a popular man, and apart from Stewart and the Rovers directors, whom he now ignored, they all seemed glad to let their reserve be demolished.

In the taxi, on the way back to the sanatorium, his vitality seemed to leave him. He sat silent, breathing a little heavily, unwontedly withdrawn, as if he were at last coming to terms with the treason of his body. "I wish I had your energy, Brian." Once, he began to cough, and the coughing grew, feeding on itself, raucous and resented, louder and louder, as though he were fighting against each new eruption. He pulled out a large, drab-green handkerchief, bending his head to it, and the bitter, private battle went on, till he relapsed, with an exhausted sigh, in his corner.

"Are you all right now, Billy?"

"I'm all right," he said, in a ghostly wheeze of a voice.

In bed that evening, his temperature had gone up to 100, but he marked it on his chart as 98·4.

"Well, did you both shout yourselves hoarse?" asked Dr Cowley. "Did the best team lose?"

"Ay, it did that," said Marshall.

"You look a bit pink," said Dr Cowley. "No double whiskies with the directors, afterwards?"

"Never touch it, doctor. Haven't touched it since I've been ill."

"Temperature down?" asked Cowley, taking the chart.

"Same as usual, doctor."

His coughing woke me in the night. I opened my eyes to the dim effulgence of his bedside lamp and saw that for the first time ever, he was using the abominated sputum mug.

"Can I get you a drink of water, Billy?"

"What?" he said, with a quick, covert turn of the head, "you

43

awake, then? No thanks, boy, I'll be all right."

Next day, instead of getting up for lunch, he stayed in bed. His temperature had not gone down; this time, he did not record it at all.

"I told you what would happen," Dr Cowley said, at last in a position of command. "Your temperature's up, you're getting sputum, and I wouldn't be surprised if you've got pleurisy as well." Yet he spoke without recrimination, as though it were sufficient for him to be right.

"Ay, I should have listened to you, doctor," Marshall said, in a slow, reflective voice, and he stared out across the room. "I'd no right to go."

"Perhaps it's taught you a lesson," Dr Cowley said. "You can't play about with this disease, even if you're a footballer. Perhaps you'll take my word for it when it's time to let you go home."

"I will that," Marshall said, half-audible.

His friends came to see him in the afternoon; Jack Grace, Dave Oliphant and Ernie Jacks. "What's the matter with you, Billy? Shamming? Don't you want to go home to the wife, then?"

"I got a cough going to Norwich, that's all there is to it. Cough and a bloody temperature." But from the strange lack of emphasis, I knew he feared there was more to it than that. He was still coughing frequently, and whenever he had to use his sputum mug, he would turn his back towards me.

"He's had the last laugh, then, bloody Stewart. If I *have* got pleurisy, I wouldn't be surprised. I wouldn't. When I cough, I can feel it there."

"Come along to the clinic and we'll have a listen to you," Dr Cowley told him. He was in their hands now, an acquiescent body to be sounded, drained, painfully rehabilitated; no better than the rest of us.

"I *have* got it, then," he said, shuffling back into the room, in dressing gown and slippers. "I can give this season up, the whole of it. They'll have to stay off the bottom without me."

"Oh, they will," I said, "they won't have to be re-elected."

"I wish I was as sure as you are."

He was entirely confined to bed now, fretting the supine days away, dabbling now in a book, now in a magazine; now putting earphones on, to listen to the radio. He spent two hours one morning in the clinic. "Sticking this in me, sticking bloody that in me," he said, kicking off his slippers with subdued disgust. "They turned me into a bloody dartboard; I thought they'd never be done. Honestly."

44

The following evening, Dr Cowley came in and said, "Your sputum's positive."

"Thanks," he said. "I'll be here with you for life, then, doctor."

"You might be," Cowley said, with his diabolical grin, and he was out of the door.

In the weeks that followed, Marshall displayed a restless stoicism. It was, as he told his wife when next she came, "me own fault, no one else's. Except Bloody Stewart, maybe, and you can't blame him, really. You can't."

His wife sat with him in melancholy silence, a double reproach now in her eyes. Once, I heard her say, "You shouldn't have gone, Billy. You know you should never have gone."

"Ay, *I* know, but it's done now. I've learned me lesson."

He was eating less, pushing his meals away with a disgust directed at his own lack of appetite as much as at the food itself. "I can't get interested, staying in bed the whole time. It's not natural."

The ritual weighing, which took place each Monday morning in the hall of the sanatorium, now became a ceremony as important to him as to the rest of us. The matron would sit beside the weighing chair, slender and pretty in her white cap and narrow, blue, archaic dress, surrounded as always by an aura of bitter-sweet unfulfilment.

"Well, Mr Marshall, is the centre-forward still carrying too much weight?"

"Too little, matron," he replied, drawing tight the sash of his red silk dressing gown, and grimly climbed into the chair. His face remained set during that silent hiatus in which the weights poised and chinked in her narrow fingers, then at last she said, 'You've lost four pounds.'

Looking at him closely, in our room, I could see his ruddy cheeks had withdrawn a little, yet I could never imagine the face being anything but robust and full.

Later that week, I was moved out of the room, to a chalet on the hillside. It was fresher there and less oppressive, a great step towards ultimate release, and yet I felt I was deserting him.

"You go, lad; good luck," he said, pushing my apologies aside. "Come out soon and join me."

"I'll try, I'll do me best." But now he seemed to speak without optimism.

I visited him every day, and knew that he was grateful; there was a sentimental core to him, however vigorously disguised: it showed obliquely and occasionally. "If you're looking for a film, *The*

45

Barretts of Wimpole Street; that's the one they ought to show. Everyone would enjoy it. Honestly."

Once, climbing the steps to the sanatorium, I met the auburn-haired woman, coming out. I think she would have liked to glide past, but I stopped her, anxious to show I did not judge her. "What do you think of him?"

She looked away, saying at last, "He's not good, is he?"

"He'll get better quick enough." I was convinced of it.

"I don't know. He's got so thin, like." Seeing him each day, it was something which had not impressed me. "Half a stone he's gone down, since I was here." I could think of nothing to say, and it was she who spoke again, at last. "I brought him a steak. Maybe they'll cook it for him." Then she was off.

After another 10 days Marshall, too, was moved from the room; to a single room on the floor above. "I asked him, 'What does it mean? Am I getting worse then?' But they won't tell you. I said 'I'm entitled to know,' I said. But they put you off, they won't tell you anything." The next day when I visited him, he told me, "They're going to collapse the other lung," and a few days after that, "I've sent my resignation in. It's not fair to the club. I won't be ready by September, not at this rate."

It was a watershed, the second, just as the moment in the taxi had been the first. He was admitting, now, that he could no longer control his future.

I went to visit him on the day they'd collapsed his second lung, but at my knock on the door a busy Irish nurse emerged, a tiny red-haired hoyden, shooing me away. "He's not to be seen by *anyone*!"

He could not be seen on the second day, nor on the third. When I asked Dr Cowley for news, he responded, with his grin, "Complications. Nothing abnormal. You look after *your* convalescence, we'll look after him."

Yet still I was not seriously anxious; that great strength, that inflexible will, were sure to see him through. On the fourth day, the nurse popped out and whispered, "You can go in for a *minute*!" Marshall was lying on his back. His face, tilted to the ceiling, seemed suddenly to have fallen away, his cheeks ravaged from within. "Is it you, Brian?" he asked, in a hoarse, husky voice. "They've really buggered me about." He stopped then and his eyes closed, but all at once he opened them to say, "Rate I'm going down, I'll be seeking re-election to the sanatorium." But when I asked him if there was anything I could get him, he replied, "Nothing, lad, nothing; it's only the after effects."

The days passed, and one's visits were still restricted. His northern friends gathered sombrely in corners, my optimism too brittle and callow for them. "They'll bloody finish him," said Ernie Jacks.

But to me, Marshall was doubly impregnable, impregnable both in himself, and because death, at 19, was something which could neither happen to me, nor to my friends. My faith was untroubled even when Marshall's wife arrived, to stay in the village.

We met now and then, sometimes in the sanatorium itself, sometimes while I was on my walks. Her suspicion of me seemed to be diminishing; as we crossed each other at the bridge one afternoon, she said, "You've been good to him. He says you go in every day," and, again, "It's his own fault, he knows it is. Headstrong, he's always the same. He ought never to have gone that day; he'd no business." She was forever bringing him something to eat – chicken, jellies, a Yorkshire pudding – coaxing the appetite which had grown so small.

"You can't even see him now," Ernie Jacks complained, coming gnome-like down the stairs, one evening, as I went up them on my way to visit Marshall. "God knows what they're up to."

It was true; they even had a notice on his door, "No Visitors Without the Permission of Matron".

I took my walks alone, now, thinking of him lying there, alone in the room, of the hollow face, the mottled hands which looked, resting on the sheet, like the broad skeleton of hands. I would walk very quickly, down the mud-tracks, across the fields, along the sea shore with its dead seaweed and myriad tiny dead starfish, thinking of the stories he'd told me, all of them implicit with his great animal force. The paradox was too huge to reconcile. Soon – after a week, perhaps, a month – the tide would turn, or rather that very force would turn it. He was a footballer and footballers like him were indestructable; I wished I could convey it to his wife, his friends, his mistress.

It was 10 days after they had made him incommunicado again that I came out of my chalet, before lunch. It was a clear March morning with a bright sun, and from the hillside, I could see far along the white road which led from the sanatorium to the village. All at once, around the farthest bend, two women came in sight, walking very slowly, side by side. It was almost a minute before I could see that one head was blonde, the other auburn, and it was only then that I knew that he was going to die.

From *The Director's Wife and Other Stories*, 1963

Child's Play

Willis Hall

The hopes I carried for my son's future as a sporting giant took another severe jolt last week when he set off for school carrying a large gold-and-off-white teddy bear. He is now coming up for seven, an age when I had expected him to go striding away with a pair of dinky soccer boots slung round his neck, or lugging a miniature cricket bag.

Furthermore, he carried the teddy bear without embarrassment and without benefit of plain cover or carrier bag. His claim that his Junior Mixed Infants School was holding a Teddy Bear Week seemed scant excuse, and served only to strengthen my doubts about modern education.

Surely, at coming up seven, Tom Brown was playing wing-three-quarter for Rugby's Second XV – to say nothing of being held over fires by older and wiser boys as part of a rigid toughening-up process? Even in these namby-pamby modern days, if I am to believe my *Sunday Times*, Michael Parkinson has a whole host of sturdy sons who tuck home goals and know exactly where silly mid-off is situated?

Where did it all go wrong, I begin to wonder?

I set the lad off on the right foot, surely to Malcolm Allison? I obtained the services of an ex-England soccer captain as his god-father. I obtained permission from a leading National Hunt jockey to name the boy after him. I should explain, perhaps, that for many years I have cherished a fantasy in which I father a boy who rushes off the Wembley turf, having captained Leeds United to F.A. Cup victory, nips into a waiting helicopter, and skies away to ride home the 33–1 outsider in the last race at Kempton. In my fantasy, the boy winks at his grizzled father on his way out of the paddock: "Try me for a fiver each way, old 'un!" Thus had I dreamed of being kept in my old age.

Again, I ask myself, where did it all go wrong? To begin with, my aspirations for the lad's racing career took a steep nosedive when he began to experience serious problems with his racing weight at the age of two and a half. On top of which, his soccer future began to look less than rosy when the very sight of a blown-up football was enough to send the lad into screaming tantrums.

When the boy was three, I put up a set of junior goal-posts in the

48

garden to egg him along. Then, as he seemed to have no talent whatsoever for kicking the ball with either foot, let alone both, I engaged the help of a friendly ex-Fulham goalkeeper who agreed to come round regularly and give him lessons between the sticks. The friendly ex-Fulham goalkeeper, being a good chum of the ex-England captain godfather to the boy, was full of enthusiasm at first, but gave up entirely halfway through the second session. My son, it seemed, had a rare gift for diving out of the way of the approaching ball.

"I'm afraid he hasn't got it, Willis," sighed my friendly ex-Fulham goalkeeper, and I have not set eyes on him from that day to this.

Not that I was deterred by early setbacks – and as witness to the fact, my cellar and summerhouse are both knee-deep in various discarded sporting equipments in midget sizes: tiny tennis racquets plus balls and net; a half-set of golf clubs cut down to size; almost all of a kiddies cricket outfit; shuttlecocks galore. There is even a miniature baseball bat, catcher's glove and Los Angeles Dodgers' cap, gifts from a kindly itinerant Hollywood restaurateur. My garden resembles an Olympic training ground for dwarfs.

My son not only ignores this panoply of sporting opportunity – he will not even venture out of doors into God's good air except under threat of physical torture.

When he arrived at the ripe old age of six, I was ready to admit defeat. After all, I am informed that Australian swimming champions are chucked into the deep end at the age of two – sink or swim. He had turned down my birthday offer of a matchball and a rowing machine in favour of an encyclopedia of prehistoric animals and a matched set of coloured ballpoints. And it was at this stage that my mind began to think in other directions. Perhaps I was being too harsh on him? For what was there in my own past sporting history for him to hook his personal star on? My four or five appearances for the regimental team in Singapore hardly qualified me for the Sportsman of the Year Award, *circa* 1953. And, if the lad did take after me, why not capitalise on it? The pen is mightier than the vaulting pole, at least as far as raking in the shekels is concerned.

I arrived at a decision. If he was not cut out to be a Billy Bremner or a Norman Hunter or an Eddie Gray – why not a Hugh McIlvanney or a Geoffrey Green or a Brian Glanville? I immediately experienced a new and pleasing fantasy:

"Hello, old 'un! Sorry to ring you at this time of night, but I've got a couple of tickets going spare in the press-box for tomorrow's

Wembley final. I'll leave them in our name at the ticket-office."

Not at all a bad parental fantasy – for starters. But if my dream was to become reality, I would have to backtrack slightly. I had got his back up about sport, and it was up to me to kindle in him a love of games. I decided upon a fatherly chat to begin with.

"Look here, son, if you've definitely decided against partici-pating in competitive sport . . ." His eyes lit up. I was off to a good start. "I honestly don't mind, but if you have definitely made your mind up that you're not going to take part yourself, why not start watching other people play football?"

"What for?" He found the idea novel if not intriguing.

"Well, now . . ." I was patience itself. "Lots of lads who don't actually *play* themselves, go along to their local grounds and watch their favourite teams play on Saturday afternoons. Or, if they can't actually *go*, they read about them or watch them on the telly. They're called fans. You've seen them standing around football grounds on *The Big Match* every Sunday afternoon." He seemed unsure, and so I added as clarification: "It comes on after Thunder-birds."

"Oh, yes." His brow cleared.

"So how about it?"

"Me?"

"Mmmm. Mmmmm. Certainly. I don't see why not."

"What do I have to do?"

"Well – choose a team. Any team. And follow it."

The above keen and intelligent sporting conversation was followed by a three day pause, after which he came up to me off his own bat and stated:

"I'm Liverpool."

"Good! Great!" I enthused. "You'll like that. There's Kevin Keegan and Stevie Heighway and we'll look in the paper together, it's called the *Classified*, and see how they've got on and so forth. . . ."

Suddenly, it seemed, a great weight had been lifted from my shoulders – had some of it come to rest, I wondered, upon the able shoulders of Bill Shankly? I bought the boy a buttonhole badge and, the very next day, he set out for school displaying it, bravely.

He came home without it.

"What's happened to your Liverpool badge?"

"I'm not Liverpool any longer."

"Why not?" I tried to keep calm.

"Because Harold Bullock, in my class, says Liverpool are crackers."

"Well, Bill Shankly doesn't think so! And what about Stevie

50

Heighway and Kevin Keegan?"

"I don't know." He shrugged. "Anyway, I'm not Liverpool any longer. I'm Leeds United."

To be absolutely honest, my heart rose. I couldn't really fault the lad for I have been a Leeds United supporter all my life. I bequeathed to him a buttonhole badge of my own and, to be fair to the lad, he wore it regularly.

A couple of months ago, I took him to see his first full 90 minutes of football. Not Leeds United, for we live in the South of England, but the local amateur team of which I am club president. We stood on the terraces together, father and son, along with a couple of hundred other stalwarts. The lad watched the game for several minutes, then ventured:

"Which ones are Leeds United?"

"Neither. The ones in the blue-and-gold are St Albans and the ones in the white are Dulwich Hamlet."

"Oh."

As far as I could gather, the answer neither surprised nor displeased him. Neither did it seem to interest him greatly. Some minutes later he drifted away from the terraces and spent the remainder of the first 45 minutes throwing Coca-Cola bottle tops at the park railings. When I looked for him at half-time he had gone home. He has never mentioned St Albans City, Dulwich Hamlet, or even Leeds United again.

So where *did* I go wrong?

The lad comes from sturdy Yorkshire stock. Is there none of that county fire in his veins similar to that which courses through the veins of Freddie Trueman or Roger Taylor or Harvey Smith?

No – none. Well, perhaps there is still hope.

Last Friday, at the end of Teddy Bear Week at his Junior Mixed Infants School, my son came home lugging back his gold-and-off-white teddy bear. The bear was sporting a rosette, having been awarded, it read, "Third Prize For Cheekiest Teddy". Did I detect a faint glimmer of triumph in the lad's eyes? I think I did.

Next year at this time he will be coming up for eight, and what then? "Second Price For Best Dressed Teddy"? And what about the year after that? "First Prize – Best Teddy Overall"! It's possible.

Yes, there is hope still. So look out, you would be Olympians for 1984. We Halls are notoriously slow-starters but when the chips are down . . .

From *Sportsworld*, 1973

Amateur Cup Final, 1956

H. E. Bates

I am very indebted to April Saturdays when rosetted legionaires invade London in their thousands and Trafalgar Square is full of men with a fine "never-been-beaten-yet" look on their sharp, lean Northern faces.

They add a new touch to the capital, robbing it of that rather stern week-day commercial air of bowler hats and malacca cane umbrellas, and tired typists running for trains.

Suddenly you feel that there is stern true business to be done, and I never drive up through North London suburbia of yellow forsythia and pink almond without hoping that the football at Wembley will match the capital's fresh taut air.

Today, when Corinthian-Casuals held a ferocious Bishop Auckland to a 1–1 draw after extra time, I need not, as it turned out, have doubted it would be otherwise. It was one of those matches which began shakily as if Wembley, rather than either team, would be the victor, and ended with fine flash and flare of trumpet for both sides.

From the kick-off it seemed as if a removal van I had seen in the morning, bearing in loud blue letters the deadly slogan "Bishop's Move", might contain in it the worst of omens for London's amateurs who, for 10 minutes, dithered against Auckland's opening attacks like a bevy of prep school-boys over-inflated by ginger beer on a wet Wednesday afternoon.

For this first opening spell you could faintly hear the creak of early doom. It was exactly as if the boys were playing the masters, and twice in four minutes the ball was skimming fiercely, as it was to do so often afterwards, over the Casuals' bar. But nervous athletes are often the best athletes and presently Casuals weathered the whip lash, pulled themselves together, grew up, became completely adult, and began to ask themselves who, after all, these North-eastern invaders were.

They began to show their weakness and their strength. Their weakness lay in the fact that their forwards were always a fraction slower off the mark and in the tackle than Bishop Auckland, and their strength in that their defence, which was to end the match in pure triumph, was a pack of lionhearts prepared to fight it out just beyond the crack of doom.

All this time it was really mostly Bishop Auckland's game. Superbly generalled, as always, by Hardisty they hardly ever fooled a pass, and their forwards, with O'Connell and Lewin always prominent, were like a pack of hounds snapping and jabbing into any hole they could find. Then, just before half-time, the whole Casuals forward line woke out of a soporific daze and gave us a taste of that clean, open, sweet football that men remember when they speak of the Corinthians of old.

Kerruish, always fast and dangerous, put in a long run; all the forwards moved like lions in a swoop on the Auckland goal: and suddenly I sensed that the battle was a long, long way from over.

So it turned out to be. The second half was only just over ten minutes old when Casuals, swooping down again, forced a corner on the right-wing from which Sharratt made a fantastically good save, almost identical with the one he had made just before half-time.

The ball went straight back to Insole for a second corner and the Essex cricket captain put over a close swinging ball that fell in the middle of a whole circus of players and a second later was in the net, put there by heaven knows whom, but probably by Citron.

The Bishop Aucklanders, hitherto as cold and tough as lumps of North Sea rock, did not care very greatly for this reverse and they showed signs, I thought, that pressure might even darken their hearts a little further.

Then, as so often happens, Hardisty began to pull them together. It is no bad business for a man to be playing at 35 as well as he played at 25, but Hardisty disdains these trivialities and not only plays as a half-back but for a great deal of the time as a sixth forward too – and there he was, prompting, weaving, scheming, pushing the ball through with immaculate beauty until, after 77 minutes play, the reward came.

The Casuals defence got itself for a second or two in one of its few painful tangles and the ball went screaming for goal. Ahm, of whom we still had not seen the last, made a magnificent save, but in a flash McKenna had the ball back in the net.

Extra time started with the same guise of impending doom for Casuals as the game itself had begun.

Oliver shot marvellously only to see Ahm bring off another splendid save, the first of so many that in the end my April-chilling fingers could no longer applaud them. From then it was no longer every "Bishop's Move".

The whole chess board was alive. The Aucklanders looked surprisingly good, and they got, if anything, better and better. But football is not, of course, all brains and feet; and the better they got the more the Casuals' spirits rose and heightened until they, too, were equally magnificent in quite another way. Ahm, in goal, the two backs, Alexander and Newton, Cowan, and the red-haired Vowels, all played, as they say, "blinders".

During this period Citron went off with a leg injury and McKenna joined him shortly afterwards. And then the strangest thing happened. In a spirited burst of inspiration every Casual forward, with Citron back, joined in a lovely movement that took the ball down to a spot that seemed as if selected by divine providence for Laybourne, just in front of goal.

Sometime in 1984 he will probably still be sitting in some Orwellian chimney corner sadly trying to remember what happened, and "look upon himself and curse his fate".

It was the golden chance every schoolboy dreams about and few men are ever given. In a moment it was lost.

"It would have been sheer robbery," said a gentleman with a

"Are you an official ticket tout? You're not on my list of fellers we roughed up last year!"

54

large and ferocious ginger moustache who sat next to me, but I could not help feeling that both sides had had, in a sense, a victory as flaming as his own wide and splendid bristles.

CORINTHIAN CASUALS: P. Ahm; F. C. Alexander, D. W. Newton; G. M. Suttleworth, R. Cowan, R. C. Vowels; D. J. Insole, J. Sanders, J. S. Laybourne, G. C. Citron, N. Kerruish.
BISHOP AUCKLAND: H. Sharratt; R. Fryer, T. Stewart; J. R. Hardisty, C. Cresswell, J. Nimmins; F. McKenna, D. J. Lewin, R. Oliver, S. O'Connell, R. Edwards.

From the *Sunday Times*, 1956

The Magnificent Seven

Tony Pawson

The Highbury career booklet for aspiring footballers begins: "Arsenal . . . Benfica . . . Ajax . . . Inter . . . Santos . . . throughout World soccer perhaps 12 clubs are truly international names recognised by every fan everywhere." Arsenal naturally will not confuse their own success story by mentioning other British clubs in the top dozen. Yet there are six more who could compete for inclusion in that list together with teams like Real Madrid. Liverpool, Leeds, Manchester United, Tottenham, Celtic and Rangers are of this stature. What in their Management accounts for achievements so widely recognised?

"Football is a simple game made unnecessarily complicated by managers. . . . A manager's success depends on how he motivates his playing staff." Both sayings come close to truth, and the best managers are uncomplicated in approach to the game, expert in their handling of men. Shankly is the elemental expression of these qualities. Liverpool's tactics are as straightforward as any in the English League. The basic rules are few. Give the pass to the nearest man. Get behind the ball when you've lost it; move into attack when you have possession; use your skill and your speed; give them no respite; chase, challenge and run at them all the time, but keeping to a zone that does not overwork you.

As so often, the style of the team reflects the strong points of the manager's own play. Shankly ran with his palms turned out like a sailing ship striving for extra help from the wind. Tireless and determined he quartered the field for Preston, a right-half unfettered by conventional position. When Joe Mercer was playing against him, a colleague whispered, "Shanks is lazy today. He's letting the left-half take his own throw-ins!"

Running on his toes like a ballet dancer he needed great strength in his calves. "I've got it still" is his proud boast, and at 60 he is able to show his players his fitness. He demands nothing of them that he did not give himself. Long before the expression "total" football was in vogue he was the totally committed footballer.

56

One of Liverpool's early heroes was Alexander Raisbeck, described as "an intelligent automaton fully wound up and guaranteed to last through the longest game on record. To watch him play is to see a man pulsating to his finger-tips with the joy of life. Swift, rapid movement, fierce electric rushes are to him an everlasting delight." That could just as well have been written of Shankly and that is the Liverpool tradition he embodies and communicates.

With this outlook his tactical talks are always positive, based on what Liverpool will do to exploit weakness in the opponents. Only once was he known to pay undue respect to the opposition. As the team gathered round his tactics table one Friday Shankly's admiration for Matt Busby and Manchester United led him to emphasise their abilities. "Denis Law, now, there's a player. Verra good with his head, and quicksilver on his feet. The man can dance on egg-shells. Watch Bobby Charlton – let him surge through from behind and ye will na' stop his shot. Ye canna' give Best an inch either. He's clever and strong. Ye can hurrt him and hurrt him, but he will keep coming." There was an anxious silence as Shankly stared at the heavy metal discs on the simulated field, red for Liverpool, white for United. Suddenly his arm sent the white spinning off the table. "That to Manchester United," he shouted joyously, "We'll sweep them off the field."

It is rare for him to so delay the punch line. One of his ways of building morale is a humorous catalogue of opponents' frailties, deliberately deriding their talent. Having seen them off their coach, he and Albert Shelley, the late trainer, would solemnly recount the depressed looks, limited abilities and unusual antecedents of the visiting team. The routine was designed to amuse, to relax and to build confidence.

Typical of his style was a conversation with Peter Thompson and Roger Hunt, his International forwards, sitting together on the bench before a match. "Dinna' be softhearted, Peter. Yon back's so scared after the fool ye made of him last time he's asked to be dropped. He's trembling in the dressing-room. But show him no pity. I'll ask a favour of you, Roger. The goalkeeper's mother is a relation of mine. She's worrit you'll break the puir lad's wrist with your powerful shooting. I've promised her you'll no' hit him, but put the ba' in the corners of the net out of his reach."

Thompson knew the back had been his master before. Hunt that the goalkeeper's mother had probably never heard of Shankly, but both felt lifted by the familiar patter.

Shankly's ability to enthuse players is obvious enough from the response. Toshack was hardly a worker with Cardiff or Cormack with Notts Forest, but they run themselves breathless for Liverpool. Six scouts from other major clubs rejected Kevin Keegan in his Scunthorpe days as lacking strength and heart. Shankly built this modest, likeable man into the most exciting of players.

Shankly is simple too in his loyalties. In his playing days he was single-minded in his belief in Preston. Tom Finney recalls in the first game he played with Shankly being driven on by shouts of "Keep fighting. We can do it yet." They were four goals down with two minutes to play.

After his managerial apprenticeship with Carlisle, Grimsby, Workington and Huddersfield, Shankly has devoted himself to Liverpool with a fervour that came to express a city's feeling. In the final stage of one League Championship Arsenal, Derby and Manchester City were all in close competition with Liverpool. Before a critical game between Manchester City and Derby, Shankly rang his old friend Joe Mercer at Manchester: "I'll be coming to your match with Derby. I hope you both lose."

There is only one club for Shankly and only one Manager who can satisfy Liverpool.

Towns react to certain kinds of Manager, certain styles of football. Liverpool and Shankly are in tune, sharing the same boisterous whole-hearted approach to life, the same passionate feeling which accepts as natural that two fans should ask for their ashes to be scattered in the goalmouth.

Shankly has no sympathy with paperwork, but types all his own letters himself. He has no love of theoretical coaching, but is the epitome of the track-suit Manager, passing on his knowledge to his players. His feel for the game and for people is instinctive and practical. Yet his and Liverpool's success stems from a thoroughness of organisation. Shankly was one of the first to have the Third and Fourth Divisions researched in depth when other Managers were somewhat scornful of their quality. Before he buys a player he will consider every aspect of his game and his personality. The approach will be oblique, but many people will be sounded out to build up the picture. And if the team has to stay in an hotel Shankly will probably have slept there before to make sure it is not too noisy or too luxurious.

One good team may make a Manager's reputation for years. But it is continuity of achievement that proves his powers. While Liverpool were winning the League twice and the Cup once in those three seasons of soaring success in the sixties he was planning the succession.

With few injuries and no failures there was little chance to experiment. No good First Division player would transfer to Liverpool to adorn the reserves. It was then that Shankly built his youth teams and bought from lower divisions. Lloyd was happy to come from Bristol in the hope of taking over in time from Yeats, Clemence to wait until he could replace Lawrence.

That policy and an unsentimental appreciation of the moment great players began to decline has kept Liverpool in the forefront for a decade.

The same judgement runs through the club. The highest transfer fee Liverpool had paid by the end of 1972 was £115,000 for Cormack. A million pounds had been spent to give modern comfort to a ground surrounded, like so many soccer stadia, by those rows of dingy redbrick houses, and the blackened walls with their scrawled graffiti. Now the contrast ideally expresses the therapeutic value of soccer, of the liberation it can bring from the dreary constraints of city life.

A professional economy of effort, a husbanding of resources for the decisive thrust, these proved profitable tactics in their accounts as well as in their play. Not one in a thousand of those crowding into Anfield on a match day would recognise or notice Eric Sawyer, the Financial Director. He is as unobtrusive as Shankly is gregarious, as in love with figures as Shankly with football. This partnership of opposites has given the club its strength. In the Second Division days it was Shankly who knew he needed players of the calibre of Yeats and St John to win the elusive promotion. It was Sawyer who recognised this was sound investment and found the £80,000 in transfer fees for them when this stretched the club resources. When Lloyd was bought, the price of £50,000 was known to be higher than hard bargaining could achieve. But to save tax it was desirable that the deal be completed before the end of the financial year.

The Secretary holds the balance between finance and football, match performance and the administration demanded of a club that has won its way to Europe for ten successive seasons.

Peter Robinson is prototype of the majority of League Secretaries in the shape of his career. Handicapped by rheumatic fever, he was watcher rather than player, but interested enough to win a job as office boy of Stockport County. Since their Secretary had no other assistance, though crowds averaged over twelve thousand, he had perforce to learn quickly the full scope of the job. Evening study took him through half the finals of the Corporation of Secretaries examinations, but a move cost him his chance to complete

59

the qualification. After his grounding at Stockport he went as Secretary to Crewe Alexander. There he was bloodied by that hectic cup-tie when Crewe, at the bottom of the Fourth Division, so nearly beat Tottenham on the way to winning the trophy for the second successive year. Robinson's memory is not of Brown's fingertip save that kept Spurs from humiliation, gave them the chance to show the difference in quality by winning the replay 13–2. It is of the overwhelming pressure of administration when a near-empty ground is suddenly flooded by a capacity crowd without the staff to cope. His education was completed by spells at Scunthorpe and Brighton. In the eight years since he was selected for Liverpool from some 250 applicants there has been no relief from the pressures of success. Yet with an Assistant Secretary, five full-time staff and extra help for Cup-ties, it is all smooth routine after that experience at Crewe. And that smooth routine, the financial commonsense with which Liverpool runs, allows Shankly to concentrate on maintaining a team that keeps the supporter on the Kop in good heart and voice.

Lancashire has usually been the dominant voice in English soccer but Yorkshire have a worthy champion to maintain the traditional rivalry.

Leeds is a club of strange contrasts. Relentlessly consistent, their record better even than Arsenal's in the thirties, they have so often failed in the crucial match. Relishing hardness, with Don Revie scoffing at the soft southerners, they have welcomed players of Eddie Gray's gazelle-like grace.

Their results were built on a steely defence yet they score goals in profusion, play with style and subtlety. Organisation and teamwork is their strength yet the club's performance centres on one man, Don Revie.

A Manager is only as good as his players. That is an over-used phrase, a half-truth at best. Certainly it is the players who win the games. But the Managers with the feel of success select the right ones, train them properly, enthuse them totally. Revie is such a Manager. Before he took over Leeds had bounced restlessly in and out of the First Division. When he was appointed in March 1961 they were near to relegation to the Third. A season later they came even closer, with only 26 points scored with but six games left, four of them away from home. They saved themselves with 10 points from those last desperate matches, their relief indulged by wild celebration on return from the final victory over Newcastle at St James's Park.

For the last three months Revie had slept little, worried continually. He would stay up late brewing tea, running over in his mind new combinations of players or tactics. Then he would lie awake brooding on how much simpler it had been as a player. It seemed inevitable to him that his career at Elland Road must be summarily ended, that he would be written off as another failed Manager. Like Shankly, he needed time, needed someone with belief in his ability. That was when the Chairman's support was vital.

Harry Reynolds, a millionaire businessman, had backed his own judgement of men in making the appointment. Revie had come to Leeds two years earlier, signed from Sunderland for £12,000. This was his fourth transfer in twelve seasons, the lower price reflecting that his International career was behind him, his playing days nearly done. Within six weeks he was made captain, the unanimous vote of the players reflecting the impact of his personality. He took over from Wilbur Cush, the little Irish inside-forward, who had found the responsibility affecting his game. Within eight months Revie too asked to be relieved of the duty, concerned at his loss of form, feeling himself an unlucky leader. Yet he still had the resilience to apply a few months later for the Manager's job advertised at Bournemouth. His request to Harry Reynolds to send the letter of recommendation brought unexpected profit. As the Chairman considered the strong points of character and experience he would underwrite he found himself thinking that these were the qualities Leeds needed in a Team Manager. "If Don is good enough to manage Bournemouth, he's good enough to take charge of our side," he told his Board. The Chairman had chosen him, so the Chairman backed him when it mattered – and with money as well as faith. For as they struggled to avoid relegation Revie was able to make the decisive purchase – acquiring Bobby Collins from Everton for £25,000. Collins, much capped for Scotland, was small and chunky, with laughing eyes, an angelic smile and the temper of a tiger. He was that mixture of aggression and cunning that Revie looked for in a footballer. At thirty-one he found new appetite for the game, began to organise Leeds in midfield until his carbon copy, Johnny Giles, took over from him.

Revie had already shown his willingness to experiment, his feel for attack, by converting Jack Charlton to centre-forward. Now in one game against Swansea he went against tradition by introducing four untried youngsters to the side – Sprake, Reaney, Hunter and Johnson. No other example better illustrates the shrewdness of his method. This was the season 1962/3 when Leeds had started to climb the Second Division, to challenge for promotion. He was free to experiment without fear. He brought them in away from home to avoid pressures if they failed. His judgement of players was proved by their performance, in that game and in the years of continuous achievement. "This is a crazy way of running the side," he told the Chairman before a match. That was no reflection of self-doubt, just a recognition that he was consciously ignoring a basic principle.

With Revie it is never change for its own sake. He prefers to build a stable side, to back it with a stable organisation, to evolve slowly once the foundation is firm. Thoroughness of organisation is the special characteristic of Leeds, devotion to detail almost an obsession.

Even in Scotland they tell a story to point the legend. For their European Cup semi-final at Elland Road Celtic needed to change stockings to avoid a colour clash. They were offered two alternatives – orange or blue. That disturbing reminder of Protestants and Rangers was taken as planned, since nothing ever happens by *accident* at Leeds.

But there is a final contradiction. In that club of hard realism there is a reverence for superstition. Revie had this feeling as a player, keeping fit on a diet of sherry and eggs for a Final in which no one else expected him to play – until Spurdle's boils confirmed his hunch. The first major trophy that Leeds won after many a near-miss was the League Cup. They were heartened when Terry Cooper dreamed he would score the winning goal against Arsenal, not even mildly surprised when he did. The players all have their good luck charms and their rituals, a whimsical preparation for their coldly calculated football. Revie himself always supervises the soap massage that is the Thursday routine, rubbing down his players as if to communicate to them something of his own personality.

Final success has so often eluded, and that is when this close relationship is most valuable, "when you have worked hard all season and have nothing to show for it at the end there is a terrible flatness. It is difficult to regenerate enthusiasm for the next match, the next season." As the dejected Leeds team trailed off behind Sunderland Revie was already telling them to forget the match and look forward to the Final of the European Cup Winners' Cup. Their consistent endeavour is a reflection of his own driving determination.

The stability of the Leeds side is matched by the backing organisation, this contribution publicly acknowledged when Don

Revie made long-service presentations to five of his staff in front of the Elland Road crowd. But there is no doubt who has built up Leeds as a club, just as their is no doubt who has built up Manchester United.

Matt Busby is synonymous with the club, the immense prestige of both suddenly shadowed by the frustrations of the past three seasons, the panic of coming face-to-face with relegation. Others might fight their way out of trouble with flailing boot, but surely not United. Other clubs might have little faith in football as a contest of skill, an expression of personality, but United surely would live or die with style. When the pressure came they behaved like just another club in trouble.

The Manager sacrificed, the lack of faith, the lavish spending, these were standard responses in a struggle for survival. The appointment of Tommy Docherty was understandable in the light of his popularity with the press and the need for a dominant character who was seen to be in charge. But the combination of Docherty, Cavanagh and Crerand clearly signalled the end of an era, the death of a tradition. There would be more emphasis on the hardness, less on the free expression and the skill that had overlaid it in the past. It took only a few weeks for that improbable headline to appear after a match at Coventry, " 'We are not animals,' says Busby".

Next it was Malcolm MacDonald complaining after the Newcastle match that Holton received the strident instruction "You've done one. Now do another." Before United had fought their way to safety the recurrent theme from press, Managers and players was of a hardness that did little credit to the club. Opinion was too uniform to be shrugged off as prejudice, especially when the past had prejudiced so many in United's favour.

Arthur Hopcraft was one of those who had rejoiced in the magic of Busby's teams and written of them with sensitive perception. Saddened by the change, he can still see it in the perspective of all that Busby achieved over a quarter of a century as Manager.

The events at Old Trafford between the summer of 1969 and the close of 1972 had a distressing shabbiness. Wilf McGuinness, a product of the famous Busby nursery of the 1950s, was callously given the responsibility of managing the players while denied convincing authority because Sir Matt stayed on in his old office, an intimidating grey eminence called "General Manager". When McGuinness failed, inevitably, he was humiliated by being returned to the reserve team as Trainer (he left the club later), and Sir Matt took the reins again. A new Manager, Frank O'Farrell, lasted 18 months before the cumulative hindrances of acrimony in the dressing-room, disfavour in the newspapers and the defection of George Best to the Never Never Land unfitted him for the job in the eyes of the Directors, of whom Sir Matt was now one. It was a sorry tale of equivocation and disavowal.

The sense of disappointment, of betrayal was evident in the acres of newsprint used to report, and comment on, the dismissal of O'Farrell and the accompanying exit of Best – off to Los Angeles and Acapulco, and Spanish sun, and nowhere. It was present, too, in all the conversation one heard on the subject in pubs, in the street, in the newsagent's. Manchester United gets a different kind of attention from that paid to any other football club in Britain. More is expected of it than from any other: more excitement on the field, more praiseworthiness, more "character". The reason for this goes back to the vision by which Sir Matt Busby began to create a team 25 years ago, and it is tied up with the personality of this man, who became the most famous and the most respected of all British Managers. And it is because Busby had made his reputation – his life, in fact – inseparable from Manchester United's that there was such a bitter regret when the club was seen to be as fallible as any other. National heroes come and go; but Busby had dominated English football from a pedestal for two generations of players.

Sir Matt's personal contribution to the game has been immense. As important as the record of success United achieved under his management is the fact that he broke new ground in extending the range of the Manager. I believe that the single quality which is common to all successful Managers, and which lifts them above the others who may be indefatigably conscientious or exceptionally shrewd, is to possess a dominant will – to possess it naturally, not to assume it. Busby always had this, and it has been of lasting significance to English football that he chose to use it not merely in composing and tutoring his teams but in aspiring in the game in a much broader sense.

His decision to build *a supply of players, not just one new side*, which would be drawn principally – *entirely*, was the ideal – from boys acquired directly from school and developed as a unit, was a daring thought 25 years ago. He was looking a long way ahead, trying to establish a plan that would give him not just his next team but one after that. Such a nursery *system*, as against looking for a gifted youngster when a Manager thought he might soon have to plug a hole in his team, is now a common-place in the League.

64

He set out deliberately to break down the barriers of status in the club. He had been a wing-half with Manchester City and Liverpool (and also Scotland's captain) before he became United's Manager in 1945, and he wanted to engender a different atmosphere from what was common in League Clubs. He remembered the dispiriting effect a young player suffered by being "just left on his own – no-one taking any interest". He saw the dangers in a situation where "the First Team hardly recognised the lads underneath . . . and the Manager was a man sitting at his desk, and you saw him once a week.

That seemed more than likely to discourage young players; and always in Busby's mind was the essentiality of encouraging talent, of urging promise into flower. He was one of the first to realise the importance of the Manager's sheer presence among his players, being involved in their ambitions and doubts so that every hint of discontent or concealed fear or unsuspected ability comes to the man in inflections of voices, flickers of expressions.

Busby was prepared to insist on backing his own judgement against Directors' views at a time when a football Manager was regarded very much as a servant of the Board – and as even a smaller minion in the eyes of the executive of the Football League. He defied the League in 1956 to lead the first English challenge for the European Cup.

It was that competition which determined Busby, and Manchester United, would give the British public surely the most emotional of all memories of football: the destruction of a brilliant young team, the fruit of Busby's youth policy, when the plane bringing the group home from Belgrade crashed at Munich airport, killing eight players; then, 10 years later at Wembley in 1968, the pictures of the ageing Busby and his captain, Bobby Charlton, who survived the crash with him, embracing in the tearful triumph of winning that trophy at last.

Between 1945 and 1968 Busby saw his teams win also the League Championship five times (seven times taking second place), the F.A. Cup twice (and twice being the beaten Finalists), and saw them consistently attract huge attendances when the public was fickle elsewhere. He was made a Freeman of Manchester and a Knight. Probably he will eventually be Chairman of Manchester United, and he has at last opened the executive of the League to the voice of a professional in the game, even if a retired professional. It is never going to be possible to dissociate Busby from the tawdry episode that injured McGuinness, O'Farrell and football itself; but his achievements stand, and they were reached by a man who aimed very high when few thought to.

65

Another who has aimed as high is Bill Nicholson. He has none of Busby's bland persuasive personality but in his gritty way an even greater dedication.

Tottenham's record under Bill Nicholson has a remarkable consistency. Since he took over in 1958 the F.A. Cup has been won three times, the League Cup twice, the "double" achieved in 1961, the European Cup Winners' Cup won in 1963, and the EUFA Cup nine years later. In his first season Tottenham finished 18th, but in the next 13 years only once were they out of the top 10. Seven major Finals were won, none lost.

That argues a meticulous preparation and a care for detail which is characteristic of his success. Nicholson has no life outside Spurs; his time and thought are wholly devoted to the club. There is still a nostalgic feeling for that side which not only won the "double" but won it with such elegance and ease. At the heart of that early triumph was the relationship between captain and Manager, between Blanchflower and Nicholson. For both it was something special and its development tells much of Nicholson and the Manager. This was how Blanchflower developed his ideas of captaincy finding understanding only from two Managers, Peter Doherty and Bill Nicholson.

I grew up with fancy ideas of captaincy. I suppose I got them from the boys' magazines. In those boyhood stories the Captain was always larger than life. He was a figure of authority and responsibility. He made decisions and changes out there on the field that dramatically altered the course of the game. And in those fantasy games that took place in my own imagination this was the kind of central figure I imagined myself to be.

On reflection, this grand fellow doesn't have much chance in reality. Perhaps he had more chance in the early days when the game began in the schools and universities. They didn't need Managers and Directors and all sorts of other officialdom to play the game.

Then came a competition of prizes and recognition of success. To win you had to get better. That demanded organisation. Somebody had to lead. As soon as they got paid to do the job there was more competition for it. So the original seat of power became dissected. The grand old Captain became a Limited Company – with Directors, a Secretary, a Manager and all. They even had a guy to carry the strip and apprentice kids to stud the boots and clean up the dressing-rooms.

66

It was thus when I came into the business as a professional. The Captain was just another player. He carried out the ball and tossed up the coin in the middle of the pitch and swore at you occasionally during play, but other than that he never seemed to have a lot of authority. At least the one's around me didn't. They were usually older players. I respected tham for their age and experience and if any of them had asked me to do something I'd have been glad to do it. But they didn't.

But as I grew older in the game and became much better at it I started to become more critical of the lack of activity around me, I wanted to get better. To get better means you must change your habits in some way. You cannot get better while keeping to the same routine. I found that to do this in a personal sense was not enough. I could change some of my own habits and improve but to continue the improvement meant that others in the team must change some of their habits too.

I tried to bring about some of these changes at Aston Villa. The Manager encouraged me. But he had no great authority at the club and as he had no clear idea of what I wanted to do he had no passionate belief in the experiments. He just wanted things to get better without any trouble from anybody. And what I was asking others to do was change their own habits – ones they felt safe and comfortable with – and some of them were unwilling to do that. I had no authority to enforce change and no desire to upset other players. We tried the experiments with those players that were willing to change and let the others train in their old-fashioned way.

Even though the team was split and the new movements restricted I found them encouraging. By trying to tackle our problems in a different way we found a new zest and belief in ourselves. By doing something different we surprised the opposition. A sequence of good results followed but we soon found it wasn't as easy as all that. The more we developed the new movements the wider we made the split in our own team. We surprised our own unwilling team-mates with the new moves as well as the opposition. This led to confusion and argument and to a growing lack of confidence among some of the willing players. Old habits that don't succeed are more acceptable. The players had lived with them for years. But new habits are expected to bring instant and constant success. If not, then why change? So the new ideas were destroyed because they had not been tried by a whole-hearted team and by a growing resentment fostered by old habits. Old habits die hard.

This led to some frustration on my part. I could not quell my natural ambitions to improve. If I could not change and improve at my club then I would just have to change my club.

This desire for change was encouraged by my fortunate experience in playing for Northern Ireland under Peter Doherty as Team-Manager.

Our sympathetic understanding made my feelings towards Villa all the more frustrating. I felt I was wasting time. I was 28. It was time to change clubs.

I joined Spurs in 1954. I had been Captain of Northern Ireland for a couple of seasons. I'd had a good grounding in First Division football with Villa. I was ready for the challenge at Spurs.

Tottenham had the great "push and run" team at their peak in the early 1950s. They were beginning to slow down and Arthur Rowe was building again. He wanted me as the new Captain. We talked about it a good deal during the transfer negotiations. I told him of my experience with the Villa players. That had taught me I must have authority on the field if I was to accept the responsibility of doing the job properly. He said he would be glad to give it to me. He wanted players and Captains who would accept responsibility.

It did not work out. By the time I had succeeded Alf Ramsey as Captain of Spurs Arthur Rowe had left the club because of a breakdown in health. Jimmy Anderson became the Manager. He had been the Assistant Manager. The job had come to him rather than him going out to look for it. He had the problem of building a new team on his hands. He knew nothing of the promises Arthur and I had made to one another during the transfer deal.

So, in time, when I found it necessary to make changes on the field of play, Jimmy Anderson and I found ourselves on opposite sides of the fence. I said I could not accept the responsibility of captaincy without the authority to act on the field. Otherwise it was just a fraud.

The changes I had made were in Cup-ties. We had been losing 3–1 to West Ham at home in the 6th round. Half-way through the second-half I changed our centre-half Maurice Norman up to inside-forward so that he could frighten the Hammers in the air. I figured that if the orthodox was not working we should try something different. It worked. We scored two goals and won the replay in orthodox fashion.

In the Cup semi-final I faced a similar problem. We were losing 1–0 to Manchester City at Villa Park. With 30 minutes to go I sent Norman up again. We went close a couple of times but we failed to score. That's when the trouble started with Jimmy Anderson.

68

The disappointment of losing a semi-final had something to do with it. So had the Press. Having little in the game to write about they chose the obvious controversy. Should the Captain make changes? It was all right when I had done it against West Ham. It had worked. But it had not worked against City. I was back to old habits dying hard.

I saw it in a different light. If the normal process was not working I reasoned that one must try something else – not something complicated that would be confusing, but something simple that every player in the team could recognise as a call for emergency stations.

I was dropped from the Spurs team. It was a convenient way of changing the Captaincy without making an issue of it. Three or four different Captains were tried in my place. Then Anderson asked me to be Captain again. I'm sure it was a genuine approach on his part. I insisted that we should announce that I had authority on the field. I would not accept the job without that. Jimmy was reluctant to make the announcement. He said I could have the authority but there was no need to make a fuss about it. I could understand his feelings and had no wish to make life difficult for him. But what if others did not understand I had the authority? What if Jimmy left as Manager? What if I tried changes and the Press or public did not accept my authority? It was a public sort of job, open to wide criticism. I was not afraid of that but I wanted it clearly understood where I stood on the matter.

Jimmy Anderson retired and Bill Nicholson succeeded him as Manager. The team was inconsistent but Bill gave most of the players on the staff a chance to justify themselves. But as the team sunk lower in the table and the fight to avoid relegation grew more frantic he eventually brought me back one night at Wolverhampton. He told me he was reinstating me as Captain. He did not have to say anything else. He had thought a great deal about it and he had made his decision that he wanted a Captain who would accept responsibility. At last the Manager and Captain were united and this had an immediate effect on the morale of the other players. We got a hard-earned point at Molineux that night and soon climbed the table to safety. Meanwhile Bill Nicholson was buying the other players who would help turn the team into a great one – Dave MacKay, Bill Brown and John White, Jimmy Greaves came later.

The paradox was that having fought so hard for the right to make changes on the field as Captain I never really had much of that to do with a great team. What need is there to make changes when things are going right? But because the authority had been fought for and generally accepted I never had any real trouble with the other players when I asked them to do something different. That did not happen often because it was rarely that an emergency happened on the field that we had not thought about and prepared for in training. If the 'keeper was hurt we knew who would take his place. If the first choice as substitute in goal was not playing we knew who was second choice. Yet, in such circumstances, if I thought someone else would have been a better substitute I could have changed this.

Only once were we caught out that I can remember. At Ipswich we lost a couple of quick goals and our defence was confused by Alf Ramsey's formation. The Ipswich wingers were lying deep and playing like inside-forwards on the wing. Their three inside-forwards were well up-field as a striking unit. Dave MacKay and I were out of touch with the men we should have been marking because we had an attacking job to do as well. Our two full-backs were in the habit of facing wingers further up-field and the confusion was too great to solve while the game was in play.

At half-time I said that Dave and I should mark the wingers because in a true sense they were playing like inside-forwards. Our full-backs could come inside and deal with the two inside-forwards.

MacKay said he would prefer to mark his own man and the full-backs thought the same. I think their pride was hurt by the confusion and they each wanted to handle their own man. Bill Nicholson suggested I should mark the winger on my side and Dave could mark his own man. We settled for this compromise but lost the match in the end by the half-time score – 3–1.

I was injured when we played Ipswich at home and they caused the same confusion. In the end they won the League title and that season we had to play them in the Charity Shield. I insisted in training that we should prepare ourselves to play them as I had suggested in the first place. Bill Nicholson agreed and that was that. We beat them 5–1. Surprise had been their greatest asset and we had robbed them of that. By training specially for it we had erased the fears of our own full-backs who had to change their habits slightly.

I go through all this detail to explain that so much depends on habit in football. That the better habits a team has the better it will be. And yet the more flexible it can be in changing its habits when the demand arises the greater that team will be.

There is no simple explanation to the relationship between the Manager and his Captain. It is like a marriage. Most of these marriages are nothing out of the ordinary. More often than not the Manager finds it difficult to pick his Captain from the players he has. He has to choose one because fashion dictates that somebody should lead the team out and carry the ball and toss the coin. And if there was one player in the bunch who had ideas of his own about authority and responsibility then most Managers would be suspicious of him. I'm sure that is how many Managers looked upon me.

One Manager of another club with whom I was friendly called me into his office one Saturday before the match. "If I came to Tottenham as Manager," he said, "the first thing I would do is call you into my office and tell you that I am the boss here."

"That's O.K.," I replied. "Then I would ask you: 'What am I?' "

"I would tell you," he said, "that *you* are nothing."

"Then I would have to say that you are the boss over nothing."

So I appreciate the part that Peter Doherty played in my development as a Captain. He did much more than accept my ambitions. He encouraged them beyond question. Thus I had great experience and confidence when I first faced Bill Nicholson as Manager.

I think Bill was suspicious of me at first. Then I think he realised that we both had the same thing at heart although we were different by nature. We both wanted the team to get better no matter how good it was. The understanding that grew between us started slowly and became very deep through the years. And as the years pass on I think we both realise on reflection that it was so much better than we realised at the time. When it was happening we were too busy to appreciate it properly.

The Manager's is a very lonely job. It is difficult for him to confide in his players because in a sense he is the master of their destiny. The Captain is one of the players but if he wants to be a great Captain he must in some way be slightly apart from them. You cannot lead them from the middle of the pack. By instinct I always tried to find a place to stand somewhere between the interests of the players and those of the Manager. I would talk about other players with Bill but I would never suggest that he pick one instead of another. I would have felt disloyal. But if he asked me which of two I thought was better I would be honest and tell him why I thought as I did.

I tried to be an example to the others in training. This was no hardship because I liked training. But this must have helped the respect grow between Bill and me. Nor did I drink or smoke. Not that these are crimes but abstinence was another common link between us. Nor was I emotional about our achievements. I did not enjoy dancing around waving trophies in the air. I accepted I had to do it for the enjoyment of our fans but I did not like doing it. I'm sure he did not like it either. His comments regarding success were always cold, much colder than mine. I was embarrassed by the boasting around us but I escaped it with humour. He gruffed his way out of it. Our satisfaction was in doing the job. We both wanted to get on with the next one.

I believe that is the reason for Bill's continued success. He sees no reason why anyone should want to rest from the job at hand. Go into his office and ask for a day off and he'll be gruff about it. He'll give you a hard time. He might not even say anything but he'll look grim. He might even give you the day off but you will leave his office feeling uneasy about it as if you'd taken the bread from his mouth. You might complain about his attitude to the others, but there is no way you could ever justify that complaint in your own mind because you know that no matter how hard you might work or how many hours you might put in that he's doing a lot more than you. You know that he is straight and honest and not making a profit behind your back.

I used to say to him: "I'm here to do the work. You are here to see that I do it." It was my way of saying that if I was going to play the game and perform the tactics then it would be better if I worked out ones nearer to my own understanding. If they proved not to be good enough then that was the time for him to interfere. If others couldn't think for themselves then he ought to be on their backs.

He did not need telling. He knew all that himself. But by keeping at everyone he kept them going much better than he would have done by easing up and expecting them to do it themselves.

We had a very special relationship. I know it. He knows it. And that's all the matters.

Bill Nicholson sees it that way too. "I gave him authority on the field, but told him always to remember two things. I had been responsible for the money paid out for the players and I took the responsibility for the results. So he must not knowingly go against my policy. It was a question of trust." Nicholson is a man you can trust.

The English League is with some reason characterised as the hardest in the world, the depth of talent making every one of the 42 games a challenging contest in a long, wearing season. But it

72

cannot be claimed as the best while English clubs have made such intermittant impact on the main European competition.

In the first 17 years of the European Cup only Manchester United reached the final in that triumphant spring of 1968.

The record is much better for the European Cup Winners' Cup with Tottenham, West Ham, Manchester City and Chelsea all winning in its first 12 seasons and Leeds making their impact this year.

But no English club can rival the record of Celtic and Rangers in these two competitions. The concentrated League programme may provide part of the explanation, since the two Scottish clubs have no such relentless pressure in their season. Yet part must be in the style and confidence of Scottish football, in the encouragement of talent and the rejection of negative tactics.

Rangers won the European Cup Winners' Cup in 1972 and have twice been runners-up. But Celtic were the European Champions of 1967, the runners-up three years later. That makes them our prime team in Europe as they have been in Scotland over so many seasons.

Jock Stein is known as "the Big Man" and he towers over Celtic's achievements, as dominant in personality as he is in physique. Yet for an Englishman the main impression is not the craggy, formidable figure, but the kindliness, the absorption in the club.

The Scots have a reputation for hospitality and Managers like Stein give this feel to a club, which is often so lacking in England. Anyone who phones the ground is as likely to get Stein himself as any other official and to have his query dealt with in person by the Manager.

Stein still has a sense of wonder at the strange reversal of fortune that transformed an unknown player into a football legend. He had been a centre-half with Albion Rovers, impressing his Manager, Webber Lees, more by his readiness to talk about the game than his ability on the field. After only three seasons he drifted out of Scottish football and into obscurity with the non-league Welsh side, Llanelli. Stein had been a pit-worker and he settled happily into that mining community until the house he kept back in Hamilton was twice burgled.

Waiting until Llanelli was beaten in the English Cup he went to tell the Manager that he would return home, give up the game and go back to the pits. Instead he was informed that Celtic wished to engage him to give experience and solidity to a team of young reserves. He left at once for Glasgow, but never played for that reserve side. Before the season started both regular centre-halves

73

were injured and Stein had to deputise in the First Team. The good players round him and the challenge of top-class football brought a new dimension to his game. He went on to captain Celtic and lead them to the Cup and League double.

His first managerial appointment was to Dunfermline, on the verge of relegation. They had not won a match for months, but they won the next five and the following season beat Celtic in the Final of the Scottish Cup. Stein had solved the difficulty of "making a provincial team think they were as good as a big city one". But once he himself went back to the big city the gulf opened wider than ever.

His career is unmatched in the history of Scottish football, yet his simple start has kept him in sympathy with the ordinary player and supporter. Typically, when a party of Welsh miners on their way to the rugby international came to look at the closed Parkhead ground it was Stein who showed them round for two hours. And when recently an away game was cancelled late it was Stein who stood by the main junction outside Glasgow flagging down supporters' coaches to prevent a wasted journey.

Stein has a great affinity for "football people", but is as happy discussing history or politics, his interests wide-ranging, but his time dedicated to Celtic. He is as open with the press as with Celtic supporters and John Rafferty has seen him work himself to exhaustion for the club.

On a March morning in 1965 the late Sir Robert Kelly announced that Jock Stein was to be the new Manager of the Celtic Football Club. Stein was but the fourth Manager of the club since it was instituted as a charitable organisation in the East End of Glasgow in 1888. Sir Robert, Chairman and son of the first Captain of the club, James Kelly, concluded an emotional occasion with the charge, "It's all yours now, Jock." Stein was to take him literally and become totally committed to the club and its players.

Not only was Stein to work himself to the point of exhaustion, travelling to keep himself abreast of what was happening in football, imparting what he had learned to his players, worrying and scheming and planning, but he became involved in their private lives, in their homes and their families: "Of course I like to win matches and win competitions but nothing gives me more pleasure than to see one of my players do well, to marry, to buy a house and to have a nice family. That's what makes it all worth while."

That was no light talk. Some were astonished recently before the club's annual Christmas party, a family affair, when Stein took charge of the gifts and labelled them, writing the names of

74

all the players' wives and their children without using a list. He knew them all.

Stein has an astonishing memory. In Lisbon, three years after Celtic had won the European Champions' Cup there, I bought an ordinary picture postcard which showed the National Stadium in which Celtic had won that cup. It was a wide view of the ground and the players were but specks on the card. There was no indication of who the contestants might be, but Stein, after a glance, said, "That's the cup final against Inter Milan." I asked him how he could know and he looked astonished. "That's the play leading up to the penalty kick," he said. "That will be right," I told him scornfully and then with some irritation he began to give names to the dots and explained that the ball went from there and to there and Jim Craig made the tackle which was punished with a penalty kick there. And it all happened three years before and he was surprised we lesser mortals had not been able to see that.

Stein worked extraordinary hours for the club. He took the training every morning, stayed on for special coaching of individuals, was interminably on the telephone at the ground and in his home, talking to football people, to Managers, to contacts, becoming satiated with the current news in the game.

He was ever available to the press, providing the routine news of the team, arguing, trying to influence opinion, putting the club's case and at times winning press friends by helping with a story on a dull day. He was up-to-the-second in newspaper office gossip, taking a delight in stirring up argument among the travelling band of reporters.

There has been recurring talk among those who do not know him well that he is a tough man. He says, "I know people think that I am hard but maybe I'm the softest of them all here." He could be right. He has never been one to dismiss the troublesome player but instead has tried to understand him. He told me once when discussing such a player, "What would he do if I threw him out, and he has a wife and family." There was a long troublesome relationship between Stein and Jimmy Johnstone; there were quarrels and suspensions, and Stein said once in exasperation, "No player has ever given me such trouble." Johnstone in a chastened mood agreed that no player could have. Stein was often advised to rid himself of the troublesome winger but he would say, "What a player he is when he plays." Johnstone was tolerated and matured under Stein's patience and settled to become a good professional and the only reward Stein wanted was to see his trickery and maybe watch him resist provocation.

75

This total involvement in the affairs of the club and all in it inevitably placed a heavy strain on the man. He never did sleep well. On trips abroad it was noticed that he was always last in bed and nobody was ever down before him in the morning. One player said of him, "He sleeps with his eyes open thinking about football."

There was the strain of long fast journeys to watch football. If there was a midweek match in England, when Celtic were not playing, in Manchester, Liverpool, or Leeds he would motor down after the afternoon's work was done in Celtic Park, talk a bit, watch the football then motor back immediately afterwards and be the first man in Celtic Park in the morning.

Such exertions were more than any man could bear and at the start of 1973 he became ill and was taken to the coronary ward of a Glasgow Infirmary for observation. He was ordered to take things easier. That was a terrible sentence to pronounce on Jock Stein.

Rangers in recent seasons have trailed behind Celtic. Their triumph in the European Cup Winners' Cup would have been all the sweeter for that had it not been marred by the unruly behaviour of some supporters. Ian Archer has observed their Manager closely.

Willie Waddell, speaking strongly into the microphone erected in the centre-circle of the Ibrox pitch, addressed 20,000 Rangers fans before the start of the 1972–73 season. It was an unusual step for any Manager to take but it was his personal contribution to football's continuing fight against the hooligan problem.

Waddell delivered in strong terms a 10 point plan – including the prohibition of drink inside the ground and a ban on all the songs of religious bigotry that can be heard whenever this club plays – and he was applauded as he left the field. This cameo illustrated graphically the difference between his job and that of any other Manager in Britain.

Rangers hold a unique position in world football and the man in charge has always been expected to concern himself as much with the club's image as with the tactical motivation of the team. Waddell, an uncompromising personality, rather typified the Rangers tradition. His single-mindedness matches that of two famous predecessors, Willie Struth and Scot Symon, who between them brought the club 25 League titles and 15 Scottish Cup victories in less than half a century.

It is doubtful whether an English Manager would seek or be given the role that fell to Waddell during that same year. When Rangers, after a decade of annual continental journeys, eventually won the European Cup Winners' Cup with a victory over Moscow Dynamo in Barcelona, that triumph was obscured by the rioting during and after the final which led to a two-year EUFA ban on the club. It fell to Waddell and not a member of the Board to fight that decision.

He did so in Brussels and the result of his impassioned plea that the players must not be penalised for the acts and indiscretions of the fans led to the suspension being halved. That was probably as important a victory as any Manager could win, for a good European season probably brings about £100,000 of gate receipts.

Shortly after this battle Waddell decided that running both the Ibrox club and the team was too much work for one man and he assumed the position of General Manager, with Coach Jock Wallace gaining promotion to the title of Team Manager. Increasingly, he saw his job stretching beyond the boundaries of the club, and he concerned himself with the politics of the Scottish game.

In February 1973, Rangers invited every other club in the country to hear their proposals for fighting the decline in gates. A hall was hired in Glasgow and again Waddell, rather than a Board member, expounded plans, which included a change in rule to deprive sides of any points from goalless draws and a series of cash prizes for the country's leading goalscorers.

It is unlikely that any other Manager would be given as wide a brief as Waddell, but few have his all round qualifications. He was a famous winger in the Rangers side that won the Scottish "double" in 1949 and 1953 and that ensures him of the affection of the fans and the respect of the players. But between serving his managerial apprenticeship at Kilmarnock, whom he took to a surprising Championship victory in 1965, he also worked as a full-time sportswriter on Scotland's best-selling daily newspaper – and not a single word was ghost-written. That experience allowed him to take a wider view of the game than many Managers whose whole adult life has been spent in the closed world of football and whose attitudes are often restricted by its sheltered nature.

Those are the six clubs who could most appropriately be added to Arsenal's list of the Internationally famous. What of Arsenal itself? The club has won the Fairs Cup, but not so far achieved the success in International competition of Celtic, Manchester United or Tottenham. Yet it is still true that Arsenal is the English club that comes first to the mind of the foreigner. In the 1930s its name echoed round Europe and the memory lingered on even in its years of depression.

Now there is justification once more for Arsenal's reputation. The present vein of success is backed by a record no other club can match (four F.A. Cup victories and four times losing Finalists, eight times League Champions, the "double" in 1971, and all achieved in the last 45 years).

Recalling his time as an Arsenal player, Joe Mercer puts high value on the tradition "You always expected to win. Even in an away game there was no satisfaction in a draw."

Its strength is not in fading memories, but in the power of organisation, in a name that attracts the young to the club and the supporters to the terraces, in a reputation to inspire pride in the players, in a bank balance to satisfy aspirations.

These were little comfort to Bertie Mee when he took over as Manager in 1966. Three predecessors had been worried into resignation by poor results, the falling gates, the burden of only the best being acceptable. Mee agreed to manage for a trial year, already clear of his priorities. Morale was his first consideration then as it remains today. He had seen a collection of talented players lack the will to knit into a talented team. There must be no more failure in the mind.

I had been impressed by the difference between the professional footballer and the professional golfer. The golfer will always produce a highly competent performance no matter whether he has just had a bad night's sleep, or flown a thousand miles, or has to play on a strange course. He knows no-one else is responsible for the figures he produces. Players are not so constant in football where one can always excuse one's own failure by blaming it on others. To win the League you need a squad of footballers who will give you 45 top-class performances out of 50. Occasional brilliance is no good over a long season. That was what I set out to impress on my playing staff, that was the response I sought. We kept and recruited those who had that attitude, the others could go.

Mee is quiet, precise, a little formal in manner, very neat in mind and appearance, not given to excessive enthusiasm. He had been one of those small nippy wingers who abounded in pre-war days when forward lines swept up five strong. Mee had been just good enough to satisfy Derby County, never good enough to satisfy his own ambition to be at the top. He was realist enough to see that he had no great career as a player even before a back injury put him out of the game. His was not a personality or a background to appeal to those who believe that footballers, coming mainly from poor homes, are more at ease with rough language and wisecracks, only respect those who have themselves been out-standing in the game. But it has been Mee's handling of men, his ability to communicate his own passion for order and excellence that has revived Arsenal.

Charlie George is the most striking example of his method. Here is a player with flashes of George Best's talent and temperament, who was as much the centre of adulation and as liable to be destroyed by it. His temper is quick to flare on the field, his comment "if they knee me, I butt them" a reflection of attitude.

Mee has integrated him into a team of workers, made him accept long periods as reserve, dealt firmly with his exuberant estimate of his own ability. That goal which won the "double" tempted George to demand special treatment. In his firm decisive way Mee made it clear that there would be no special treatment, that the club was always more important than the individual and if George knew a better one he was welcome to go there.

Always polite with the press, Mee protects the players from publicity, never revealing a private interview, never encouraging the sensational story.

When Arsenal won the "double" it was only on the Monday night before the Cup Final that they made sure of the League. Mee was quick to exploit the advantage. With one title safe there was less tension. Concentration on the League had kept them free from worry over the Final, aloof from its preliminary pressures. Liverpool had had it on their minds for three weeks and were still involved in interviews on the morning of the match. Mee made his players unapproachable for 48 hours, was not surprised that the quiet preparation gave them the strength in extra time to outrun a team noted for its fitness.

Fitness is no fetish for Mee, just the expression of his technical competence as a physiotherapist. He was in the Army at 20, his football maintained by guest matches for Southampton and a representative Wanderers side in the Middle East. At his own request he went to the Army physiotherapy school and learnt enough to complete his civilian qualification. Out of the game at 27, he made a new career in the Health Service, running remedial centres, one of them at Camden Town.

Organising the F.A. Treatment of Injury courses at Carnegie College and Lilleshall kept him in touch with the game and in 1960 he came to Arsenal as their physiotherapist. That gave him six years to note what he would do if he was Manager. His second priority was to get the best Coach in the country. The choice was Dave Sexton for his technical knowledge, his ability to be inventive and sustain interest in routine training, for the respect in which he was held by his players.

Safeguarding the future was the next consideration, unusually expressed by cutting out one of Arsenal's four teams, their Metropolitan League side. This was no cost-saving measure. The aim was to give all young players the chance to come through quicker to high-class football, to make more rapid decisions on whether they had the necessary potential for Arsenal. Good organisation, quick decisions are the essence of Mee's style, and nowhere was this more important than in the scouting system. He took on Gordon Clark as Chief Scout, a former Manchester City player, who had later established a reputation at West Bromwich Albion for his ability to unearth young talent. Clark was out of a job at the time, but had the qualities Mee appreciates. His mind is a filing cabinet of players' statistics, his enthusiasm takes him to seven or more games a week, his judgement of ability has other clubs consistently phoning him for his opinion.

Mee, the organisation man, has built a highly successful method team within the disciplined framework of a club whose standards are rather special. I once asked him if he regretted letting go Forsythe, the Scottish full-back who was with Arsenal as a youngster. He looked surprised: "It doesn't follow that because you are an International you are good enough for our squad." There was no more to be said about Arsenal.

From *The Football Managers*, 1973

Necessary Screwballs

Michael Parkinson

Goalkeepers, like things that go bump in the night, defy analysis. They are as much a mystery in the general order of things as the function of the human appendix. It is, of course, relatively easy to explain what they have to do: their purpose is to prevent the ball entering the net by any means at their disposal, namely by catching it, punching it, kicking it, heading it or, if they so desire, throwing their caps at it. The mystery lies in the fact that this seemingly simple, straightforward task produces people of incredibly complex and often eccentric personality. Even today, when the game appears to be played by robots, when individuality is ruthlessly stifled at birth, the goalkeeper has survived with all his personal idiosyncracies intact. No one knows better than goalkeepers themselves that the price they pay for their freedom is to be talked about behind their backs. In the totalitarian regime of modern-day soccer they are treated as necessary screwballs. Because of this it is a commonly held belief that all goalkeepers have a slate loose, that the nature of the job being what it is a man must be barmy to do it. The other theory is that the goalkeeper, because he is custodian of the most important part of a football field, slowly develops into a paranoiac.

I suspect that Clakker May would be regarded as a classic example by those people who reckon all goalkeepers are born crazy. You'd never suspect there was anything wrong by looking at him. He was a tall, stringy, quiet youth who lived with his parents and 10 brothers and sisters in a council house near the pit gates. He became our goalkeeper quite by chance. One day we were a man short, and Len, our trainer, asked Clakker to play in goal. The result was a revelation. It wasn't so much when he donned the jersey he changed in his attitude towards his team mates, it was simply that he believed that the rules of the game related to everyone except himself.

We became aware of his quirk the first time he touched the ball. He left his goal line to meet a hard, high cross, caught the ball cleanly, shaped to clear downfield, and then, for no apparent reason, spun round and fled to the back of the net. This move dumbfounded players, officials and spectators alike. As we stood gaping, Clakker ran from the back of the net and booted the ball over the halfway line. Nobody moved as it bounced aimlessly towards the opposite goal and then the referee broke the silence by blowing on his whistle and pointing to the centre spot. This appeared to upset Clakker.

"What's tha' playin' at?" he asked the referee.

"I was just about to ask thee same question," said the referee. By this time Len had run on to the field.

"What the bloody hell . . ." he began.

"Nay, Len. Tha' sees I caught this ball and then I looks up and I saw this big centre forrard coming at me and I thought, 'Bugger this lot'; so I got out of his way," Clakker explained.

"Tha' ran into t'bloody net wi' t'ball and tha' scoored," Len shouted.

"Scoored," said Clakker, incredulously.

"Scoored," said Len, emphatically.

Clakker shook his head. Len tried to keep calm. "Look, lad," he said, putting his arm round Clakker's shoulders, "I know it's thi' first game and all that, but tha' must get one thing straight. When tha' catches t'ball gi' it some clog downfield. Whatever tha' does don't run into t'net."

Clakker nodded.

But it made little difference. In the next 20 minutes Clakker ran into the net 13 times and we were losing 14–2. At this point the referee intervened. He called us all together and said: "Na' look, lads, this is making mock of a great game. If it goes on like this t'scoor will be in t'hundreds and I'll have to mek a repoort to t'League Management Committee and there'll be hell to play." We all nodded in agreement. The referee thought a bit and then said, "What we'll do is amend t'rules. If Clakker runs into t'back of t'net in future it won't count as a goal, allus providin' he caught t'ball on t'right side of t'line in t'first place."

Everyone agreed and play continued with this extra-ordinary amendment to the rules. At the final whistle we had lost 15 to five and Clakker had shown that apart from his eccentric interpretation of the rules he was a remarkably good goalkeeper. Nobody said much after the game. It seemed useless to ask Clakker what went wrong because all of us agreed that like all goalkeepers he was a bit screwy. Our theory was confirmed by Clakker's old man, who when told of his son's extraordinary behaviour simply shook his head and said, "He allus was a bit potty".

But that was not the end of Clakker's career, not quite. He was picked for the next game because we didn't want to hurt him too much. Len, the trainer, called us together on the night before the game and explained how we might curb Clakker's madness. His plan was that the defenders should close in behind Clakker whenever he went out for a ball and bar his way into the net. Any resistance from Clakker should be firmly dealt with and if possible the ball taken from him and cleared upfield. In case Clakker should break through his own rearguard Len had taken the precaution of hiding the nets. His theory was that provided Clakker ran into goal, but straight out again, the referee would be unable to decide what had happened.

The reports of our last game had attracted a large crowd to the ground for Clakker's second appearance. All his family were present to see if it was true what people were saying about Clakker's extraordinary behaviour.

Things worked quite well for a time. Every time Clakker caught the ball we fell in around him and urged him away from his goal. Once he escaped us and nipped into goal, but he had the sense to escape immediately around the goalpost and clear downfield. The referee looked puzzled for a minute and gave Clakker a peculiar look, but did not give a goal because he could not believe what he thought he saw. We were leading two goals to nil with five minutes of the first half left when Clakker gave the game away. Overconfident at having duped the referee once before, he ran over his own goal line with the ball. His plan came to grief when he collided with the iron stanchion at the back of the goal. As he staggered drunkenly against the support the referee blew for a goal and gave Clakker the sort of look that meant all was now revealed.

When half time came none of us could look forward to the next 45 minutes with any optimism. Len came on the field and beckoned myself and the centre half to one side. "Na' look, lads, we've got to do something about yon Clakker," he said. "I've thought about playing him out of goal, but that's too dangerous. I can't just take him off because yon referee wouldn't allow it. So there's only one thing we can do." He paused and looked at both of us.

"What's that?" I asked.

"Fix him," said Len.

"Fix him?" I said.

Len nodded. "When you get a chance, and as soon as you can, clobber him. I don't want him to get up, either," said Len.

The centre half was smiling.

"Look," I said to him, "we can't clobber our own team-mate.

83

"You're holding up the game . . ."

"Get him off or I'll book you!"

"*He's badly hurt! . . . Shouldn't be moved . . . !*"

"*Callous —— . . .*"

It's not done."

He looked at me pityingly. "Leave it to me," he said. "I've fixed nicer people than Clakker."

It took two minutes of the second half for Clakker to get fixed. There was a scrimmage in our goalmouth and when the dust had cleared Clakker lay prostrate on his goal line. Len came running on to the field, trying to look concerned. The centre half was trying hard to look innocent. Clakker's father had drifted over to the scene and was looking down at his son's body. "He's better like that," he said.

Len said to him, "Tek your Clakker home and don't let him out till t'game's finished."

Clakker's old man nodded and signalled to some of his sons to pick Clakker up. The last we saw of them they were carrying Clakker out of the field and home. We did quite well without him and managed to win. Afterwards in the dressing room some of the lads were wondering how Clakker became injured. Len said: "Tha' nivver can tell wi' goalkeepers. It's quite likely he laid himself out."

Clakker had a profound effect on me. Since that day many years ago when he was persuaded out of the game I have never been able to watch a football match without spending a great deal of the time wondering what was going on underneath the goalkeeper's cap. None of the goalkeepers I have ever seen in first-class football could hold a candle to Clakker, but most of them from time to time have revealed flashes of rare individuality. Bradford Park Avenue once had a goalkeeper called Chick Farr who thought nothing of racing far out of his goal area, tackling an opposing forward and racing off downfield like a demented Stanley Matthews. Whenever his little fantasy was interrupted by a successful tackle Farr would gallop back to his goal line, from time to time casting fearful glances over his shoulder like a man being pursued by a ghost. Farr's other party piece was strictly illegal. When he could not be bothered to save a high shot he would reach nonchalantly above his head and pull the cross-bar down. Faced with the inevitable telling off from a referee, Farr would pull his cap down over his eyes and try his best to look gormless. His act was a convincing one, not because he was born that way, but because like every goalkeeper he had become expert in hiding his folly. Occasionally, however, the stresses of the occupation became too much for some goalkeepers and they crack up. Sometimes it happens in public, as with the recent case of a First Division goalkeeper who showed his displeasure at the way the crowd was criticising his

86

goalkeeping by taking his shorts down and showing a large part of his backside to the terraces. At least, this particular goalkeeper relieved himself in one great, spectacular gesture. The majority of his kind spend years suffering between the posts, whipping boys for the mob at the back of the goal, sacrifices to the inefficiency of their team-mates. I watched one goalkeeper at Barnsley suffer this way through many seasons. He came to the club fit and virile and stuffed with confidence. When he left on a free transfer he had shrunk inside his green jersey, his nerves were destroyed, they even rumoured that his wife had left him. I often wondered what became of him and discovered the truth sometime later when I was doing a story about a building site. I was talking football with the foreman when he asked me if I remembered the goalkeeper. I said I did and the foreman said he was working on the site.

"Where is he?" I asked.

"Up theer," said the foreman, pointing towards heaven. "Where exactly," I enquired, hoping he wasn't trying to be funny.

"On top of yon chimney," said the foreman.

I peered up, and there, high in the sky, sitting on top of the chimney was the goalkeeper.

"He seems to like it up theer. Can't get him down until it's knockin'-off time," said the foreman.

I thought there might be a story in it, so I asked the foreman if I might interview the goalkeeper.

He shrugged. "He's a funny bugger, but I'll try."

He cupped his hands to his mouth and bellowed at the top of the chimney, "Alf, theers a repoorter down 'ere what wants to interview thi abart goalkeepin' ".

There was a long silence. Nothing stirred on the top of the chimney for a while and then the figure turned and looked down. And down the miles of silence separating us floated the reply:

"Tell him to get stuffed."

The foreman shrugged and said, "I told you. He's a rum feller. Still, I always think tha's got to be a bit strange to be a goalkeeper."

I've often wondered since what kind of peace the goalkeeper discovered on top of that chimney, and wondered also what kind of revenge he was planning on the people below who had driven him there. I don't think he was potty or excessively anti-social. It was simply that he, like every goalkeeper, knew what it was like to be one of the world's most abused minority group.

From *Football Daft*, 1968

West Germany v. England, 1970

Geoffrey Green

The World Cup drifted away from England in the Guanajuato Stadium here today and now they are left with a private sense of emptiness and a desolate sadness. Two goals up with only 20 minutes left, and Bell and Hunter substituted for Charlton and Peters at that point, they had both feet, so it seemed, in the semi-final of this ninth global football championship.

It looked all over. But it never is so against these Germans. The day of settlement for that 1966 final had to come some time and it came now, dramatically and in extra time – as indeed there had been at Wembley four years ago.

In an admirable resurgence of spirit, stamina and skill the Germans earned a win that seemed at one point far beyond their reach. Drawing level at the end of normal time it was an old-fashioned move that finally drove the last blade in for victory, five minutes into the start of the second period of the extra half hour.

Grabowski, beating Cooper for speed on the outside, moved to the by-line and centred deep to the left. Up went Lohr to head back square and there was Muller to grab his ace goal of these championships as he volleyed home from close range. Never perhaps will he or his side treasure a goal more deeply.

That was it, the end of a remarkable battle royal in the midday sun which was finally a cruelty to man. England's guns were covered then, though they fought to the last inch and the last seconds to rescue their cause with shots by Mullery and Newton which dipped just over the German bar and a miscue by Ball as Hurst headed down to his feet.

Yet the better side won in the end. And they won because, once Beckenbauer had put the Germans back in the match when it was three-quarters gone, England wrongly proceeded to pull in their horns, pack the perimeter of their penalty area and concede the central areas to the twin German generals, Beckenbauer and Overath, supported by that wise old owl, Seeler. That was the heart and core of this extraordinary upheaval when all seemed done.

Meanwhile the future holds every germ of possibility. The semi-finals next Wednesday will be between Germany and Italy on the one hand and Brazil and Uruguay on the other. It was a neat division of world power: Europe against South America. It will be a struggle between different ways of life and playing football.

At the end Helmut Shoen, the German manager, said: "I never gave up hope of my side even when they were two down and once we had pulled one of those back and raised our game I did not think we would lose. But it was a magnificent match."

If Sir Alf Ramsey, in his disappointment followed with the words: "I have never seen England give away two such goals", I would not know which ones he meant. This may seem cruelly ungracious to anyone who had to suffer out there in the sun. But I do feel that Gordon Banks, had he been under England's crossbar, would not have come off his line to let Seeler's header loop over him and that he would have cut out Lohr's cross header that led to the winner by Muller. But all that is now in the past.

Having travelled 170 miles by road yesterday from the turbulent concrete jungle of a million-strong city of Guadalajara, England moved to this charming little provincial centre, a place by comparison drowsy and closely wrapped. Already, in a week, the Germans, champions of their eliminating group, had made it their temporary home. With their black, red and yellow banners and their song of "Deutschland Ueber Alles" they were now challenged by the invading English clans. But, all told, it was quieter, more inviting.

When the teams came out, England in red and Germany in white, there was an echo of that sunny Wembley final of July, 1966. England now, sadly, were without Banks their master goalkeeper, sick overnight. In his place stood Chelsea's Bonetti. On the field were five men on each side who had contested the last World Cup Final, but now there was something special. This was Bobby Charlton's 106th cap for England, to beat Billy Wright's record set up 12 years ago.

The English and the German games are alike in character. Both are full of control and this we saw as the first half hour unwound, with England's 4–4–2 against Germany's 4–3–3. In spite of that supposed mathematical superiority in midfield by Moore and his men it was, in fact, Germany, through the offices of the great Beckenbauer, Overath and Seeler, who began to dominate no-man's land.

It was a fascinating duel in the sun, spiced by firm, hard tackling and a physical challenge wedded to ball control. It was not the

Brazilian game and within the opening 20 minutes both Lee – for the second time in three appearances – and Muller were booked by the Argentine referee.

England, by their quick breaks and concentration of numbers in the important places at the right time, held these Germans, with Moore marshalling superbly as usual and Charlton, Ball, Mullery and Peters breaking with the tide.

At the 31st minute one of these breaks paid off handsomely as England took the lead with a magnificent goal. Mullery began the move in midfield with a long cross pass to Newton, left to right, and then was up to glide through a crowded German goalmouth to hook home a rasping shot to the top corner from some eight yards. It was unstoppable. Mullery, the creator, was also the executioner – Alpha and Omega.

Germany began the second half with Schultz in their defence in place of Hottges. By the quarter hour, too, they had replaced Libuda, on the right flank of attack, with Grabowski. By then England had played both Germany's old fashioned wingers out of the game, but, more important, by that moment England were two up.

Their second goal came after only four minutes into the second period. Again it was a quick break from defence into attack, a spring being uncoiled. At one end there was the monumental Moore to rob Seeler and start the move.

From Moore the ball sped between Ball and Hurst and there again was Newton, gliding in on the blind side from the right, to pitch his cross towards the far post, where Peters, also an unsuspected ghost, floated in to strike the ball home. At that the old chant of "You'll never walk alone" split the skies from the English sectors on the packed banks. It might have been home again.

But these Germans are never finished, as we have learned before. So often they seem able to pull something special out when their backs are to the wall. Now it took an individual effort by Beckenbauer, the elegant ball-player who seldom seems to change his pace, to rekindle Germany's flagging hopes. With 20 minutes to go he picked up a rebound from Lee, nosed his way past Cooper and, with a cross shot from the right hand edge of the penalty area, beat Bonetti's dive to the far corner. That was 2–1.

Now perhaps came one of the turning points. With 12 minutes left a fine move between Peters and Ball saw Bell cross to the near post and there was Hurst's diving, glancing header to roll a mere inch past the far post with Maier stranded.

Yet Germany were not yet finished. With the clock showing only eight minutes to go Fichtel crossed from the left diagonally and there was little Seeler, who seems to live on spring heels, to go get behind Labone and plant a looping header to the far top corner, catching Bonetti off his line. Like Wembley four years ago, it was extra time once more.

ENGLAND: P. Bonetti; K. Newton, T. Cooper, A. Mullery, B. Labone, R. Moore, F. Lee, A. Ball, R. Charlton (sub., C. Bell), G. Hurst, M. Peters (sub., N. Hunter).

WEST GERMANY: J. Maier; H. Vogts, H. Hottges (sub., W. Schultz), K. Schnellinger, K. Fichtel, F. Beckenbauer, W. Overath, R. Libuda (sub., J. Grabowski), U. Seeler, G. Muller, L. Lohr.

From *The Times*, 1970

Distillery Days

Derek Dougan

It is amazing how important Boys' Club football was in Belfast. It reared many prominent Irish internationals and famous English and Scottish League club players. Players of note who came from Boyland Youth Club were Jimmy Nicholson and Jacky Scott. The greatest player after my time who came from Cregagh was, of course, George Best.

When I was with Cregagh Boys' Club, I signed for Distillery Football Club. I was 15 years old at this particular point, but I already had some connections with two other clubs in Belfast. Linfield had signed me when I was 14 and I went up to Windsor Park and trained religiously, two nights a week, for months and months. I didn't make any progress and didn't play for any of their teams and I left, rather disillusioned. I was, however, playing well for the Boys' Club team at the time. I was captain, and my position was inside-left. I had once set my heart on playing for the Glens because I followed them devoutly for years and years; ever since I was 10, in fact. Coming from the east side of Belfast, I thought it should be my ambition to play for Glentoran. They sent a scout to watch me and he reported that I wasn't a bad ball player. But I couldn't make their fourth team, which was rather ironical, because a couple of years later I was playing against the Glens in the Irish Cup Final when I was on the winning side and got an Irish Cup winner's medal. One of the reasons why I was emotionally involved with the Glentoran ground was that just after the war, about 1946, I used to go there with some of my school friends to catch tadpoles and, as we called them, "smicks". The Oval then was one large bomb-site with craters – the result of what was inflicted on "loyal Ulster" because of its Britishness and its wartime value to Britain. In a few years it was transformed back to a football ground, with thousands of people coming to watch. In those years I got the bug for playing football, and when I went back to the Oval as a 13-year-old I couldn't believe what had happened.

Where I had spent a number of years as a seven-year-old catching tadpoles and "smicks", suddenly there were 22 men running about and performing with virtuosity and artistry. It was a built-in nostalgic feeling, a feeling of great sentiment, to see all this coming about within a few years. When I was a little boy I had five heroes, Sammy Lowry, Sammy Ewing, Sammy Hughes, Tim Williamson, and outside-left "Dado" Feeney, from Londonderry. When I was watching those "famous five" playing, I had the impression – and it stayed with me for a long, long time – that Sammy Lowry was the most fantastic outside-right I had ever seen. Sammy Ewing was the best "killer" of the ball with his chest that I had ever seen. I never saw Tommy Lawton or the equally famous "Dixie" Dean play, but I am certain that if I had I would still have wished that I could head a ball like Sammy Hughes. Even to this day, I sometimes wish that. Surely Sammy Hughes was the most brilliant header of the ball I have seen in my life.

Distillery F.C., which I joined when I was 15 had a manager then called Jimmy Macintosh, the former Blackpool and Preston Scottish International. Distillery Street lies off the Grosvenor Road, and the football ground is situated at the bottom. Behind it, the Distillery itself produces Irish Whiskey (not Scottish, Whisky). It is also situated not too far from the Falls Road which borders on both Protestant and Catholic communities, and those teams that I played for in the middle fifties were mixed sides of Protestant and Catholic players. We also had two or three Scots over, and even they were mixed – Scottish Protestant and Scottish Catholic. I certainly never found any problem with religion in my Distillery days. We had mixed sets of players and we also had a mixed set of spectators, coming from both areas. I can't remember any sort of trouble involving the two sides of the community in those days, and it's pleasant to look back, especially with the situation as it is now.

When I was playing for Distillery – a "mixed" team – Linfield were firm in ruling that everyone employed by that Club should be Protestant. In early days Ulster was largely Scottish, its settlers of, say, 300 years ago nearly all coming from Scotland, hence names of streets near our house like Thistle Street. So far as football is concerned Linfield follow the same traditions as Glasgow Rangers and even play in exactly the same colours.

It is ironical how things have worked out for me because the situation could have been reversed and I could have been playing for Linfield after all. When I was prominent as an amateur player, and holding my place in Distillery Football Club, I know for a fact that I could have signed as a professional for Linfield. One team that I don't remember much about, apart from what I have been told, was Belfast Celtic. They were mainly a Catholic stronghold, and they played at Celtic Park in Catholic surround-ings. They had to go out of existence in the late forties for political reasons.

93

My first game for Distillery was about my sixteenth birthday, when I played against Glenavon in the Irish Cup. I suppose when you are always used to playing in front of a handful of spectators any real "gate" looks big. The gate I played in front of that day was about £300! This way of putting it seems rather strange to anyone living outside Belfast, but that was how they judged the crowd there. They didn't say it was 5,000 or 10,000 people watching today, they said that the gate money was £300 or £600. In Ulster the money that was taken at a match seemed more important than the number of people who watched.

The nickname for Distillery was the "Lilywhites", the reason being that we played in white jerseys and black knickers – the same colours then as Preston North End, Tottenham Hotspur and the English International team. Looking back our colours seem to have been more or less "neutral" amid those that aroused more of love and hate.

All that seems far, far away when I remember my visit to Grosvenor Park in October 1971, on the day before Northern Ireland played Russia. I went from the city centre, up the Grosvenor Road and down Distillery Street, with the military all around. I remember how the Oval had been destroyed by the known enemy during the last world war. I saw what remained of Distillery Football Club from the vicious actions of an unknown enemy. But on the bit of stand that was still there, I read in clear, large letters: "Distillery F.C., 1879". So long was the tradition that had gone up in smoke.

From *The Sash He Never Wore*, 1972

Fizz It About

Michael Carey

Poor Sir Alf couldn't understand England's defeat by Italy at Wembley. You are not alone, Sir Alf.

The padded cells of this island are filling up with people who no longer understand football or the utterances of those who play, manage or administer it.

Sitting alone at Port Vale this week and marvelling at the wit and wisdom of their manager ("There is nothing wrong that two or three successive wins would not put right") it struck me that what the game needs now is a sharp injection of simplicity.

Never mind people like Jimmy Hill making it easy for morons like me to understand. Football, and particularly the England team, needs managers with the endearingly uncomplicated mentality of the likes of Ivor Powell.

Asked to explain his success at Bradford City, Powell once revealed: "We have a wonderful harmonium in the dressing room." His team, he confided, trained on a frugal diet except after matches, when they were permitted "steaks with all the tarnishings."

We need people like the late Joe Smith, of Blackpool, who according to his players gave only one pre-match team talk in his life. He said memorably: "Don't hang about in the bath afterwards, lads, we're catching the 5.20."

We need people like Johnny Carey, who whatever the state of the game invariably said to his team at half-time: "Fizz it about, lads! You'll be all right as long as you fizz it about."

We need people like the Derby County director who went up to his team's leading scorer after a goalless first half and said, confidentially: "If you get a chance this half, Jack – score!"

We need people like the unknown Fourth Division manager who gave his forward line a fearful rollicking and concluded by saying: "You're shooting from too close. Shoot from further out, then they'll dip under the bar."

We need people like the former manager of Bradford Park Avenue, who strode into the dressing-room at 2.55 one Saturday, alive with invention, and told his team: "I think we'll play 4–3–3 this afternoon."

We need people like the well-known present-day manager who

once told me: "With one more player, there'll be an overnight transaction in this team."

Simplicity itself, you see. No mind-bending phrases like environmental awareness, peripheral vision, blindside running, left-flank strikers and high morale players.

So don't worry too much, Sir Alf. Perhaps it's not the game that's changed, only the words.

From *The Observer*, 1973

One More Time

Danny Blanchflower

The first time I saw him at Wembley he was a raw kid in the other team. In those days, he wore the same numbered shirt as I did and as we waited for the royal introduction I looked him over.

He looked neat and proud and a little nervous in his royal blue tracksuit with his name, Frank McLintock, embroidered across his heart.

The Duchess of Kent noted that, too. "The other team have their names on their suits," she said as I introduced my team-mates to her.

"Yes, ma'am," I said, not wishing to be outdone, "but *we* all know one another."

We knew one another well enough in those days to have beaten Leicester eight times out of 10, and we felt that this game was not going to be the odd one or two.

It was a match easily forgotten and after the final whistle I was too busy carrying the Cup to note what happened to Frank.

A couple of years later he was back at Wembley with Leicester again. He made no great impression on the game, his team losing to Manchester United. It was Law, Crerand, Quixall and Herd who took the eye.

But I watched Frank and his team-mates walk back down the tunnel with their loser's medals. They looked like they were crawling into a hole in the ground to bury themselves.

"It was a terrible feeling," he told me later. "Your parents and family are all there, hoping you'll win. You come off the field not believing it's all over and you've lost."

After Frank was transferred to Arsenal I met him on the tube one day with Ian Ure. They talked about their disappointments at Highbury and how they wanted things to get better. I recall similar feelings of my own and I thought Frank's ambitions, too, might work out for him.

Some years passed and there he was at Wembley again, in a League Cup Final for Arsenal against Leeds. He walked off with another loser's medal.

The year after that he was back again in the same competition against Swindon. Arsenal lost 3–1 and Frank could not explain that to himself. "That was the worst one," he will tell you. "When you added it all up, there was no way that Swindon could win. We had 20 corners to their three. I had not seen Don Rogers before, but even so, how could they beat us 3–1?"

Four times at Wembley and four times a loser. Frank was not sure whether he was lucky or unlucky. "You feel lucky to have been there so often but you wonder why you have not won just once."

On reflection, he believes he chased shadows in those days. "I was running about trying to do everybody's job. I was too impulsive."

By the time he got to Wembley for the fith time in 1971 his shirt had been changed from 4 to 5. The Monday before the Cup Final his team had clinched the League Championship in a fine game at Tottenham. Now, as Arsenal captain, he was ready to follow the path I had taken when I first saw him at Wembley back in 1961.

I watched him carefully, noting his performance and behaviour with approval. His side won in extra time. He had captained a second team to the double in this century. Ours was an exclusive society and I welcomed him into it.

The following year he lost at Wembley yet again, against Leeds. Six times and just one precious win. At the time I thought that would be the end of it.

His team were beginning to crack and, as the old-timer, he was the first they would think of replacing. He lost his place and asked for a transfer, not really wanting to leave Arsenal, but to enjoy his last years as a player in a first team somewhere. He then won his place back and he had no thought of moving.

It was a bitter shock when he found he had been placed on the transfer list at the end of the season. "I'm an emotional person," he says, "and I was hurt. I suppose if Arsenal had been doing well and I had now been with a bad team I would have felt bitter about it. But how can I?"

He was talking in the visitors' bar at Loftus Road after Queen's Park Rangers had pipped an unfortunate Coventry in the last kick of a most exhilarating Cup-tie.

How, indeed, could he think anything but good of his transfer from Highbury to Shepherds Bush? He and Terry Venables seem to have a partnership like that of Paul Newman and Robert Redford in "The Sundance Kid" and "The Sting". Frank, at 34, is still a talented player, wiser now, diplomatic and handsome, enjoying his last years in a different team, one more entertaining to watch.

"When I was at Highbury I could not understand criticism of our team," he added. "I don't necessarily agree but I can understand it better now. Coming here has opened my mind."

And so the years have passed and Wembley seems to be calling him back again. Supposing Rangers overcome his old team, Leicester, in the next round and carry on to Cup Final day?

Can you not imagine the Royal introduction?

"You've been here before?"

"Yes, ma'am . . . it's now seven times."

From the *Sunday Express*, 1974

Bad Guy Turns Good Guy

John Moynihan

On a bleak January morning 11 years ago, a metallic built 19 year old hardly exceeding five foot five inches in height with red hair capping an almost angelic baby face presented his employers Leeds United with a transfer request. The reason for young Billy Bremner's desire to leave Elland Road said the new manager, Don Revie, at the time was his "homesickness" for Scotland.

The incident made only a few paragraphs in the national Press and Bremner, encouraged by Revie, stayed on at Elland Road. Now Bremner, at 30, and on the threshold of a year which could bring him the moon, the stars and anything else he cares to put in a claim for, can look back on that transfer request with some amusement.

In his testimonial year, which will be capped by a match at the end of the season at Elland Road, there seems little reason to doubt the League championship trophy will be displayed at his benefit. There are also such other "wee" trophies as the F.A. Cup and the U.E.F.A. Cup to be won: Leeds will surely be somewhere around at the kill in both.

Then around the time of Wimbledon and strawberries and cream at Henley, Bremner will lead Scotland into the World Cup finals in West Germany. On recent evidence he will be captaining a side with an outside chance of winning the cup instead of being simply a tartan stooge for the more gifted teams.

The change in Bremner's fortunes would certainly make good copy in a children's fairy story. After last season's Cup final against Sunderland, some critics claimed his partnership with Johnny Giles was finished and the "wee fella" himself was over the hill.

Then came news of the Leeds suspended fine for rough play by the Football Association.

But as soon as the new season began, Bremner and his side radically changed their image. It was like Attila the Hun deciding to give up fighting for sculpture and making it to the Louvre.

Bremner is personally delighted at the change – although it

certainly took a long time coming and long may it reign. "You know, I can see now what people were getting at when they complained about dissent," he now reflects. "It really was reaching unbelievable proportions. Yes, I know I was perhaps the biggest culprit – but I realise now it was as stupid as everyone said. I've talked to one or two players at other clubs this season and they seem to agree with me. Now that Leeds have cut out dissent completely, we are much better for it."

Bremner says he is "enjoying the game more this season than for quite a few years – Leeds are a better side and the way we are playing is good for the game. I hope everyone will take a leaf out of our book."

This marked change of attitude plus his sudden passage from being a very good player into a great one has delighted his two managers, Don Revie and Willie Ormond.

Revie, who was inside-right for Leeds on the January day in 1960 when the tiny Bremner made his debut on the right wing, was full of praise for his captain after the U.E.F.A. Cup match against Hibernian.

"Playing a sweeper's role, he gave possibly the finest individual performance I have seen in all my years in the game. We thought we knew all there was to know about him but, at Easter Road, he showed us yet more facets in his incredible make-up."

Ormond was equally ecstatic after Bremner's performance against Czechoslovakia and West Germany: "Billy is playing better than ever," he told me. "I think the change came in the match we lost 1–0 against England at Wembley. He's never looked back since then. He's having a great season, a player second to none.

"He's improved so much since he lost all that impetuosity. He was always flying off the handle. Mind you, he always went out there and did his best for Scotland, but things often didn't go as well as they are now."

Bremner made his 651st appearance for Leeds against Derby yesterday including 495 league games. Nobody is more pleased and relieved about his change of image than his fellow professionals, many of whom suffered during the blustery, belligerent sixties when English soccer reached a new sickening level in playing conduct. Sometimes Bremner seemed more intent on making enemies than friends.

He had arrived at Leeds from his native Stirling, a city noted for its castle and carpets, as a young lad after playing for the Gown Hill Juniors.

He won schoolboy, under-23 and full international caps but the headlines in the early Leeds days were usually for cautions and suspensions.

One image clearly comes to mind of Bremner descending like a voracious falcon on to the backs of a group of struggling zebras (i.e., representatives of Manchester United and Leeds). His first cap was against Spain in 1965 and he was described then as being a "prince of nigglers".

The crux came when he was sent off in 1967 for fouling Grummitt, the Nottingham Forest goalkeeper. Revie was furious and Bremner began to mellow from then on.

"Well, he was a bit *loud*," says Dave Webb of Chelsea, who almost broke Bremner's heart after scoring the winning goal in the 1970 Cup Final replay. "But Billy's so much more mature now. He was always a great professional but now he's added something extra. I remember him coming into the Chelsea dressing room after we had won and congratulating us."

Bremner's temperament off the pitch has also become more level-headed. He was noted in the past for making the odd embarrassing remark to the representatives of foreign teams. They were meant to be humorous but weren't.

Bremner's sense of humour was at its best when he spoke after being awarded the Footballer of the Year Award, 1970. And come to think of it – he could win that award again too. What a year it could be for the red-headed prince from Stirling.

From The Sunday Telegraph, 1974

Sound Advice
To The Young

Derek Dougan

When some big-wig comes to a school to present the prizes and gives a speech about the importance of tradition, you can tell by the glazed looks in the eyes of his young, captive audience that no one really knows what he is talking about.

The word "tradition" is supposed to be self-explanatory, one of those respectable words that no one is expected to challenge. It can cover a multitude of sins. We can carry on doing stupid things, saying this is how they have always been done as a matter of tradition. "What was good enough for my grandfather was good enough for my father, what was good enough for my father is good enough for me."

Today young people are rebelling against traditional systems and attitudes. They are not so easily impressed by the way things were done in the past.

In professional soccer a great many "traditions" have been swept aside, not always without a struggle. Until 1961 there was a traditional system which kept players tied to a maximum wage. They were bound to a kind of feudal system, which was common in other spheres of life until the industrial revolution. Our own revolution was fought in the law court.

In the game itself traditional styles of play have altered radically. The old two–three–five system was so well established that even now many supporters think in terms of two full backs, three half backs and five forwards when their teams are thinking simply of defenders, midfield men and strikers.

I know supporters who think there's something wrong with a team that doesn't have two wingers, upfield waiting for the ball, and criticise Sir Alf Ramsey for not relying on speedy wingers in the England side. They yearn for the days of Matthews and Finney, forgetting that the pattern of play, influenced by European football, has changed and that forwards must now do their bit in defence.

There is another kind of tradition that goes far beyond playing systems and administrative procedures.

An outward sign of it can be found in showcases at successful grounds throughout the country. Neatly set out behind locked glass panels are the trophies and shields, the cups and mementoes accumulated over the years. *En masse*, they look either impressive or absurd, depending on your view of these collections.

I have known youngsters coming into the game to pass such showcases with hardly a glance. They mean nothing to them. As silverware, it may not be worth as much as the traditional corporation plate in the local town hall. As a tangible reminder of achievements, its value is more abstract.

Some clubs, like museums which hoard most of their treasures in the basement, have stacked away their prizes for lack of room. But it's not a case of them being out of sight, out of mind. A club which has won a heap of trophies over the years takes on a strange aura. Players sense it in the atmosphere, even without gazing at the trophies.

My first experience of this was when I arrived at Aston Villa, by way of Portsmouth and Blackburn. It was like joining a Guards regiment after being with the RAOC. At first the atmosphere was overpowering. I was with a great club and it's not easy to live up to such greatness. At the same time I enjoyed the stimulus and the challenge. It wasn't until later, after I had left Villa, that I realised the peril of leaning too much on tradition.

Tradition can obscure reality. Villa was so mesmerised by past glories that they could not see what was happening to them until it was too late. Tradition was romanticised, a fatal mistake.

Wolves' traditions are not so closely related to the dim and distant past. They were largely established in the fifties, in European football – a dynamic tradition of fast, hard-hitting, attacking football, the foundation laid by Major Buckley and built on by Stan Cullis.

I think we need a perceptive psychologist to relate the ability and achievements of a player to the club he represents. It could be that a player has to search for and find his club as a man finds the right woman to marry. Each of us has traditional gifts, qualities or characteristics formed early in life, at home or school, influenced by parents or teachers who were themselves influenced by earlier traditions.

Why does a player who has failed to make the grade with one club succeed with another?

After all, he is playing the same game according to the same rules on the same sort of pitch. The reason may be in the need for a player's personality to fit the traditional personality of his club.

When there is a clash between his outlook and the club's, never the twain shall meet.

A player has to feel "comfortable" with a club for him to do his best. I am sure there are players who are better with obscure, nondescript clubs than they would be with conspicuously traditional clubs because they do not have the personalities to measure up to the demands handed down from the past.

There is no need for such a player to feel ashamed about this. In Michael Parkinson's television programme, Dirk Bogarde, an accomplished actor, admitted he would be hopeless in traditional, Shakespearean plays. To each his own

On the other hand there are players who need a traditional atmosphere to sustain them, and going to clubs of less renown, they would lapse into mediocrity.

Speak of tradition and certain clubs spring to mind – Manchester United, Spurs, Arsenal – and not all of them in the First Division. Preston, Notts County, and original or early members of the Football League are aware of their traditions, which serve as an incentive for them to fight their way back to the top.

We should neither despise tradition nor over-rate it. When it becomes an excuse for complacency it is harmful. When it inspires teams to greater efforts it is a force with which an opposing team has to reckon.

From *Derek Dougan's Book of Soccer*, 1973

The Match

Alan Sillitoe

Bristol City had played Notts County and won. Right from the
kick-off Lennox had somehow known that Notts was going to lose,
not through any prophetic knowledge of each home-player's
performance, but because he himself, a spectator, hadn't been
feeling in top form. One-track pessimism had made him godly
enough to inform his mechanic friend Fred Iremonger who stood
by his side: "I knew they'd bleddy-well lose, all the time."

Towards the end of the match, when Bristol scored their winning
goal, the players could only just be seen, and the ball was a roll
of mist being kicked about the field. Advertising boards above all
the stands, telling of pork pies, ales, whisky, cigarettes and other
delights of Saturday night, faded with the afternoon visibility.

They stood in the one-and-threes, Lennox trying to fix his eyes
on the ball, to follow each one of its erratic well-kicked movements,
but after 10 minutes going from blurred player to player he gave
it up and turned to look at the spectators massed in the rising stands
that reached out in a wide arc on either side and joined dimly
way out over the pitch. This proving equally futile he rubbed a
clenched hand into his weak eyes and squeezed them tight, as if
pain would give them more strength. Useless. All it produced was a
mass of grey squares dancing before his open lids, so that when they
cleared his sight was no better than before. Such an affliction made
him appear more phlegmatic at a football match than Fred and
most of the others round about, who spun rattles, waved hats and
scarves, opened their mouths wide to each fresh vaccillation in the
game.

During his temporary blindness the Notts' forwards were
pecking and weaving around the Bristol goal and a bright slam
from one of them gave rise to a false alarm, an indecisive rolling of
cheers roofed in by a grey heavy sky. "What's up?" Lennox asked
Fred. "Who scored? Anybody?"

Fred was a younger man, recently married, done up in his
Saturday afternoon best of sports coat, gaberdine trousers and
rain-mac, dark hair sleeked back with oil. "Not in a month of
Sundays," he laughed, "but they had a bleddy good try, I'll tell
you that."

By the time Lennox had focussed his eyes once more on the

players the battle had moved to Notts' goal and Bristol were about to score. He saw a player running down the field, hearing in his imagination the thud of boots on damp introdden turf. A knot of adversaries dribbled out in a line and straggled behind him at a trot. Suddenly the man with the ball spurted forward, was seen to be clear of everyone as if, in a second of time that hadn't existed to any spectator or other player, he'd been catapulted into a hallowed untouchable area before the goal posts. Lennox's heart stopped beating. He peered between two oaken unmovable shoulders that, he thought with anger, had swayed in front purposely to stop him seeing. The renegade centre-forward from the opposing side was seen, like a puppet worked by someone above the low clouds, to bring his legs back, lunge out heavily with his booted foot. "No," Lennox had time to say. "Get on to him you dozy sods. Don't let him get it in."

From an animal pacing within the prescribed area of his defended posts, the goalkeeper turned into a leaping ape, arms and legs outstretched, then became a mere stick that swung into a curve – and missed the ball as it sped to one side and lost itself in the folds of net behind him.

The lull in the general noise seemed like silence for the mass of people packed about the field. Everyone had settled it in his mind that the match, bad as it was, would be a draw, but now it was clear that Notts, the home team, had lost. A great roar of disappointment and joy, from the 30,000 spectators who hadn't realised that the star of Bristol City was so close, or who had expected a miracle from their own stars at the last moment, ran up the packed embankments, overflowing into streets outside where groups of people, startled at the sudden noise of an erupting mob, speculated as to which team had scored.

Fred was laughing wildly, jumping up and down, bellowing something between a cheer and a shout of hilarious anger, as if to get his moneysworth on the principle that an adverse goal was better than no goal at all. "Would you believe it?" he called at Lennox. "Would you believe it? Ninety-five thousand quid gone up like Scotch mist!"

Hardly knowing what he was doing Lennox pulled out a cigarette, lit it. "It's no good," he cursed, "they've lost. They should have walked away with the game" – adding under his breath that he must get some glasses in order to see things better. His sight was so bad that the line of each eye crossed and converged some distance in front of him. At the cinema he was forced down to the front row, and he was never the first to recognise a pal on the street. And it spelt ruination for any football match. He could remember being able to pinpoint each player's face, and distinguish every spectator around the field, yet he still persuaded himself that he had no need of glasses and that somehow his sight would begin to improve. A more barbed occurrence connected with such eyes was that people were beginning to call him Cock-eye. At the garage where he worked the men sat down to tea-break the other day, and because he wasn't in the room one of them said: "Where's owd Cock-eye? 'Is tea'll get cold."

"What hard lines," Fred shouted, as if no one yet knew about the goal. "Would you believe it?" The cheering and the booing were beginning to die down.

"That goalie's a bloody fool," Lennox swore, cap pulled low over his forehead. "He couldn't even catch a bleeding cold."

"It was dead lucky," Fred put in reluctantly, "they deserved it, I suppose" – simmering down now, the full force of the tragedy seeping through even to his newly-wedded body and soul. "Christ, I should have stayed at home with my missis. I'd a bin warm there, I know that much. I might even have cut myself a chunk of hearthrug pie if I'd asked her right!"

The laugh and wink were intended for Lennox, who was still in the backwater of his personal defeat. "I suppose that's all you think on these days," he said wryly.

"'Appen I do, but I don't get all that much of it, I can tell you." It was obvious though that he got enough to keep him in good spirits at a cold and disappointing football match.

"Well," Lennox pronounced, "all that'll alter in a bit. You can bet on that."

"Not if I know it," Fred said with a broad smile. "And I reckon it's better after a bad match than if I didn't come to one."

"You never said a truer word about bad," Lennox said. He bit his lip in anger. "Bloody team. They'd even lose at blow foot-ball." A woman behind, swathed in a thick woollen scarf coloured black and white, like the Notts players, who had been screaming herself hoarse in support of the home team all the afternoon was almost in tears at the adverse goal. "Foul! Foul! Get the dirty lot off the field. Send 'em back to Bristol where they came from. Foul! Foul, I tell yer."

People all around were stamping feet dead from the cold, having for more than an hour staved off its encroachment into their limbs by the hope of at least one home-team win before Christmas. Lennox could hardly feel his, hadn't the will to help them back to life, especially in face of an added force to the bitter wind, and a

108

"You're bad news, Willie. Celtic lost at home today."

goal that had been given away so easily. Movement on the pitch was now desultory, for there was only 10 minutes of play left to go. The two teams knotted up towards one goal, then spread out around an invisible ball, and moved down the field again, back to the other with no decisive result. It seemed that both teams had accepted the present score to be the final state of the game, as though all effort had deserted their limbs and lungs.

"They're done for," Lennox observed to Fred. People began leaving the ground, making a way between those who were determined to see the game out to its bitter end. Right up to the dull warbling blast of the final whistle the hard core of optimists hoped for a miraculous revival in the worn-out players.

"I'm ready when yo' are," Fred said.

"Suits me." He threw his cigarette end to the floor and, with a grimace of disappointment and disgust, made his way up the steps. At the highest point he turned a last glance over the field, saw two players running and the rest standing around in deepening mist – nothing doing – so went on down towards the barriers. When they were on the road a great cheer rose behind, as a whistle blew the signal for a mass rush to follow.

Lamps were already lit along the road, and bus queues grew

quickly in semi-darkness. Fastening up his mac Lennox hurried across the road. Fred lagged behind, dodged a trolley bus that sloped up to the pavement edge like a man-eating monster and carried off a crowd of people to the city centre with blue lights flickering from overhead wires. "Well," Lennox said when they came close, "after that little lot I only hope the wife's got summat nice for my tea."

"I can think of more than that to hope for," Fred said. "I'm not one to grumble about my grub."

"'Course," Lennox sneered, "you're living on love. If you had Kit-E-Kat shoved in front of you you'd say it was a good dinner." They turned off by the recruiting centre into the heart of the Meadows, an ageing suburb of black houses and small factories. "That's what yo' think," Fred retorted, slightly offended yet too full of hope to really mind. "I'm just not one to grumble a lot about my snap, that's all."

"It wouldn't be any good if you was," Lennox rejoined, "but the grub's rotten these days, that's the trouble. Either frozen or in tins. Nowt natural. The bread's enough to choke yer." And so was the fog: weighed down by frost it lingered and thickened, causing Fred to pull up his rain-mac collar. A man who came level with them on the same side called out derisively: "Did you ever see such a game?"

"Never in all my born days," Fred replied.

"It's always the same though," Lennox was glad to comment, "the best players are never on the field. I don't know what they pay 'em for."

The man laughed at this sound logic. "They'll 'appen get 'em on nex' wik. That'll show 'em."

"Let's hope so," Lennox called out as the man was lost in the fog. "It ain't a bad team," he added to Fred. But that wasn't what he was thinking. He remembered how he had been up before the gaffer yesterday at the garage for clouting the mash-lad who had called him Cock-eye in front of the office-girl, and the manager said that if it happened again he would get his cards. And now he wasn't sure that he wouldn't ask for them anyway. He'd never lack a job, he told himself, knowing his own worth and the sureness of his instinct when dissecting piston from cylinder, camshaft and connecting-rod and searching among a thousand-and-one possible faults before setting an engine bursting once more with life. A small boy called from the doorway of a house: "What's the score, mate?"

"They lost, two–one," he said curtly, and heard a loud clear-sounding door-slam as the boy ran in with the news. He walked with hands in pockets, and a cigarette at the corner of his mouth so that ash occasionally fell on to his mac. The smell of fish-and-chips came from a well-lit shop, making him feel hungry.

"No pictures for me tonight," Fred was saying. "I know the best place in weather like this." The Meadows were hollow with the clatter of boots behind them, the muttering of voices hot in discussion about the lost match. Groups gathered at each corner, arguing and teasing any girl that passed, lighted gas lamps a weakening ally in the fog. Lennox turned into an entry, where the cold damp smell of backyards mingled with that of dustbins. They pushed open gates to their separate houses.

"So long. See you tomorrow at the pub maybe."

"Not tomorrow," Fred answered, already at his back door. "I'll have a job on mending my bike. I'm going to gi' it a coat of enamel and fix in some new brake blocks. I nearly got flattened by a bus the other day when they didn't work."

The gate latch clattered. "All right then," Lennox said, "see you soon" – opening the back door and going into his house.

He walked through the small living-room without speaking, took off his mac in the parlour. "You should mek a fire in there," he said, coming out. "It smells musty. No wonder the clo'es go to pieces inside six months." His wife sat by the fire knitting from two balls of electric-blue wool in her lap. She was 40, the same age as Lennox, but gone to a plainness and discontented fat, while he had stayed thin and wiry from the same reason. Three children, the eldest a girl of 14, were at the table finishing tea.

Mrs Lennox went on knitting. "I was going to make one today but I didn't have time."

"Iris can mek one," Lennox said, sitting down at the table.

The girl looked up. "I haven't finished my tea yet, our dad." The wheedling tone of her voice made him angry. "Finish it later," he said, with a threatening look. "The fire needs making now, so come on, look sharp and get some coal from the cellar."

She didn't move, sat there with the obstinacy of the young spoiled by a mother. Lennox stood up. "Don't let me have to tell you again." Tears came into her eyes. "Go on," he shouted. "Do as you're told." He ignored his wife's plea to stop picking on her and lifted his hand to settle her with a blow.

"All right, I'm going. Look" – she got up and went over to the cellar door. So he sat down again, his eyes roaming over the well-set table before him, holding his hands tightly clenched beneath the cloth. "What's for tea, then?"

His wife looked up from her knitting. "There's two kippers in the oven."

He did not move, sat morosely fingering a knife and fork, "Well?" he demanded. "Do I have to wait all night for a bit o' summat to eat?"

Quietly she took a plate from the oven and put it before him. Two brown kippers lay steaming across it. "One of these days," he said, pulling a long strip of white flesh from the bone, "we'll have a change."

"That's the best I can do," she said, her deliberate patience no way to stop his grumbling – though she didn't know what else would. And the fact that he detected it made things worse.

"I'm sure it is," he retorted. The coal bucket clattered from the parlour where the girl was making a fire. Slowly, he picked his kippers to pieces without eating any. The other two children sat on the sofa watching him, not daring to talk. On one side of his plate he laid bones; on the other, flesh. When the cat rubbed against his leg he dropped pieces of fish for it to eat on the lino, and when he considered that it had eaten enough he kicked it away with such force that its head knocked against the sideboard. It leapt on to a chair and began to lick itself, looking at him with green surprised eyes.

He gave one of the boys a sixpence to fetch a *Football Guardian*. "And be quick about it," he called after him. He pushed his plate away, and nodded towards the mauled kippers. "I don't want this. You'd better send somebody out for some pastries. And mash some fresh tea," he added as an afterthought, "that pot's stewed."

He had gone too far. Why did he make Saturday afternoon such hell on earth? Anger throbbed violently in her temples. Through the furious beating of her heart she cried out: "If you want some pastries you'll fetch 'em yourself. And you'll mash your own tea as well."

"When a man goes to work all week he wants some tea," he said, glaring at her. Nodding at the boy: "Send him out for some cakes."

The boy had already stood up. "Don't go. Sit down," she said to him. "Get 'em yourself," she retorted to her husband. "The tea I've already put on the table's good enough for anybody. There's nowt wrong wi' it at all, and then you carry on like this. I suppose they lost at the match, because I can't think of any other reason why you should have such a long face."

He was shocked by such a sustained tirade, stood up to subdue her. "You what?" he shouted. "What do you think you're on wi'?"

Her face turned a deep pink. "You heard," she called back. "A few home truths might do you a bit of good."

He picked up the plate of fish and, with exaggerated deliberation, threw it on the floor. "There," he roared. "That's what you can do with your bleeding tea."

"You're a lunatic," she screamed. "You're mental."

He hit her once, twice, three times across the head, and knocked her to the ground. The little boy wailed, and his sister came running in from the parlour. . . .

Fred and his young wife in the house next door heard a commotion through the thin walls. They caught the cadence of voices and shifting chairs, but didn't really think anything amiss until the shriller climax was reached. "Would you believe it?" Ruby said, slipping off Fred's knee and straightening her skirt. "Just because Notts have lost again. I'm glad yo' aren't like that."

Ruby was 19, plump like a pear not round like a pudding, already pregnant though they'd only been married a month. Fred held her back by the wrist. "I'm not so daft as to let owt like that bother me."

She wrenched herself free. "It's a good job you're not; because if you was I'd bosh you one."

Fred sat by the fire with a bemused, Cheshire-cat grin on his face while Ruby was in the scullery getting them something to eat. The noise in the next house had died down. After a slamming of doors and much walking to and fro outside Lennox's wife had taken the children, and left him for the last time.

From *The Loneliness Of The Long-Distance Runner*, 1959

Innovations

Alan Simpson

It is customary at the beginning of each season to look back on the season before. It seems to me that the most interesting things that happened last year were the many suggestions to improve the game for this year.

We started off one year with the new offside law in the Watney Cup. You could only be offside in your opponents penalty area! I look forward to the development of this. Nine players on each side forming a guard of honour round each others penalty area with one player on each side fighting for control of the midfield.

This changes the whole concept of the ideal midfield player. Anyone who can run 35 miles in 90 minutes. I confidently predict that Dave Bedford will be the first £1,000,000 player in 1975. Strikers will work out at £25 each, or five for £100.

We had a very interesting suggestion from the American Football Association. They find the most difficult problem in selling the game in the States is the lack of goals scored. Your American football fan can't be doing with the 0–0's, the 1–0's and the 2–1's. He wants the 9–8's and the 15–14's after extra time. And so the American F.A. have suggested to F.I.F.A. that the size of the goals should be increased. They suggest that instead of eight yards by eight feet they should be 10 yards by 10 feet.

Fine, why not? Hampton are quite prepared. Already our manager is scouring the local recreation grounds searching for a 7 foot 10 inch goalkeeper. Naturally, our professional colleagues can't wait that long. Requisite training for a first division goalkeeper these days is two hours a day in the torture chamber at the Tower of London. Four circuits of the moat and 10 turns on the rack have worked wonders for Peter Shilton. How many of you noticed on *Match of the Day* against West Ham how he pulled his socks up without bending down?

But why stop at 10 yards by 10 feet? Why not have the goal stretch from one corner flag to the other? It might cost a few bob in nets but it would make interesting reading in the *Sunday People*. "After 10 minutes of the first half George Armstrong scored Arsenal's 34th goal with a six inch inswinging corner kick that crept in by the near post with the goalkeeper floundering just outside the penalty area." Why don't the American F.A.mind their own business?

I was also intrigued by a suggestion from the Canadian F.A. Instead of sending players off for the duration of the game, they suggest we incorporate a "sin-bin" as in ice-hockey. Five minutes for obstruction, 10 minutes for tripping, 35 minutes for a punch in the ear-hole, and 85 minutes for suggesting the referee might have made a slight error of judgement in giving offside. After the appropriate time is up the player can come back on the field. The only snag is that it requires, as in ice-hockey, an electronic clock to decide when each individual penalty has been served. Consequently, to be fair, the clock must be stopped whenever the ball goes out of play. Consequently, the average game of football would last for five hours. Consequently, all the players would be knackered half way through the first half. Consequently games kicking off at three o'clock in the afternoon wouldn't finish until eight o'clock in the evening. Consequently, our bar takings would be cut in half, so as far as I'm concerned the Canadian F.A. can go and get...... ! I beg your pardon, I didn't mean to be offensive.

I discount rumours that the Chinese F.A. have suggested we should play across the park with the goals situated each side of the halfway line.

I also retain an open mind on the reported recommendation

"Blimey, you wouldn't think it was the same bleedin' match. . . ."

from the Israeli F.A. that the pre-match stud inspection should be carried out by a fully qualified Rabbi with authorisation to remove up to half an inch of any stud over the permitted length.

There are one or two innovations I should be happy to see take place, if only for the convenience of the spectators. I like the idea of the illuminated scoreboard in cricket – a light comes on under the number of the player who fielded the ball. What about illuminated numbers on the backs of players? A goalmouth scramble… who put it in? Suddenly the number on his back lights up! He runs back to the middle, arms in the air. He steps in the puddle in the centre circle, there's a puff of smoke, the floodlights fuse and the substitute comes on. Hmmm, perhaps not. We haven't got that many goalscorers at Hampton.

I think the self-retrieving toilet roll might do us a favour though. A goal is scored! The toilet roll is thrown onto the pitch, a press of a button, and it rolls itself up and comes back into your hand – just like those things you blow into peoples faces at parties.

You don't fancy it? Well, never mind, it's better than the suggestion by the Italian F.A. No more tackling and defenders must stand 10 yards off the ball when the opposing forwards are in possession. Still, I suppose it was to be expected – three minutes after Egypt invaded Israel, Italy surrendered.

From *The Hampton Football Club Programme*

Liverpool Star

Hunter Davies

The look on Steve Heighway's face after the 1971 FA Cup Final
was something you rarely see in football. Liverpool had been
beaten by Arsenal, and it was the end of their world, their life,
their purpose. Their dressing-room contained the hulks of ship-
wrecked souls. Smith and Toshack had become dehumanised. It
was best to avert your eyes. Yet there was Heighway smiling an
eager, boyish, excited, glowing smile.

In 1971, Steve Heighway was something that rarely happens in
football. He'd arrived as a complete outsider, straight from
university, brought up in a middle-class home, untrained and
uncoached, a free and natural spirit, not a battery-farm footballer
who'd been force-fed from the age of 13. He might just as well have
landed from Mars.

It wasn't, therefore, surprising that he was excited. He would
have liked to have won, but as a normal human being, the pleasures
of the occasion had not been wasted on him. He's now had three
full seasons as a Liverpool star. Has he ceased to be a normal human
being, and become a footballer?

"It all happened so suddenly that first year. I didn't know what
was happening. Until that year I'd never had the slightest intention of becoming a professional footballer. All I wanted to be was a
teacher."

He'd just graduated from the University of Warwick, getting
a second in politics and economics, and was about to do a teachers'
course. One day he got a phone call at his digs in Coventry to
say that some Liverpool scouts had seen him playing for the British
Universities, and that the manager was coming to see him in
person.

"I was completely unimpressed. It was nothing to do with my
life. Mr Shankly came and went on about all the money I'd
get as a first-team player. I said, "Oh yes, but your reserve players,
how much do they get?" He wouldn't talk about me being in the
reserves.

"I was about to get married, and my wife was even less impressed
than I was. But we decided that even on a reserve player's salary
we could buy a house – something we'd never manage for years on a
teacher's pay. It might be interesting for a couple of years to do

something else. I'm not a confident person. I didn't expect to succeed. I never do. I took it for the money.

"Looking back, I was very naive that first year. I just went my merry way. If I had a bad game, I thought, 'Too bad.' I carried on as I'd always done, messing around, not facing problems seriously, being a bit of a clown.

"I realise now the team didn't like me that first year. I probably knew it at the time, but never worried about it. I was probably rather aloof."

The fruits of his three years of success are easy to see. He has a large detached £20,000 house beside the sea at Ainsdale, near Southport. He and his wife, who's a primary-school teacher, both have cars. His income is 10 times what he'd be getting as a teacher.

But he's by no means flash. They have a two-year-old son, Jamie, and all three take a simple camping holiday each year. He saves rather than spends, and thinks footballers are not paid enough compared with other entertainers.

That's the first sign that the process of footballisation has had an effect on Mr Heighway. There are many others. Like almost all footballers, he hates the football Press.

"In the football system they are the weak link. They've never played football, and they know nothing about it. That first year they were saying nice things, even though I knew they were getting it all wrong. When they said nasty things, I was very hurt, even though I knew they were still getting it all wrong.

"I decided that as neither the good nor the bad was true, I should give them up. For almost three years, I've never read the back pages. I think the standard of popular sports reporting is disgustingly low. The serious papers get it all wrong by over-complicating what is a simple game. I have no confidence in any soccer reporter to write about soccer.

"I never watch our matches on TV either. I know how I've played on Saturday. I know my mistakes. I want to get away from it. TV can't make you a better player.

"The reaction to out defeat by Red Star was typical of the fickleness of the Press and public. No one could call them a great side. All we didn't do was take our chances. I think the criticism of England's defeat by Poland was equally unfair.

"A soccer reporter should not try to entertain or amuse but to inform but they can't. They don't understand what it's like to play soccer."

Heighway now knows what it's like to be in the public eye, in good times and in bad, which is why he has such sympathy for all players. And like all players, he's also found that what happens *inside* a club is hardest of all.

"It's the huge emotional ups and downs I can't take. There's an enormous high created when you win, but three days after I feel washed out. I begin to doubt my capabilities. The happy moments don't last long. Then, when we lose, I feel consumed with guilt and worries. It's not a natural thing, being a professional footballer.

"At the same time, there's the physical strain. It drains you completely. You should see the lads on a Monday, especially towards the end of a season. Their backs are aching, they can hardly stand up.

"I sit on the coach after a match and think, I'm packing it up. I wasn't fitted for this game."

Naturally enough, he now feels part of the team. They're relaxed with him, having been through so much together. He still doesn't play cards, except when requested to make up a hand, but he knows exactly why they play. They find the boredom of travelling unbearable. He still prefers to chat or read.

Rather surprisingly, he's not particularly close to Brian Hall, Liverpool's other graduate, though they're friends. His three closest friends in the team are Keegan, Cormack and Boersma. He's now one of them, for better or for worse.

His wife thinks it is for the worse. She says he's changed in the three years, become harder, less sensitive. He thinks he probably *has* changed. He certainly worries more. Even though he's now an insider, he can see only too clearly what the system does to its players. The normal player accepts it, having known nothing else.

"A manager is paid to get the team on the field, and secure the best result. That's his job. But there *must* be other ways of getting good results. I don't really want to go into the manipulation of people, but that's what it is.

"In other forms of management, there is an attempt to handle each person in a different way. Football managers are untrained as managers, and they know only one method, total dedication, because that's what they have. In a way, the worst sort of footballers become managers. Only the fanatical would be silly enough to do it. They have to have the drive of Hitler. Our guy never lets you relax. The constant need is to win trophies. He never lets up.

"The right way to manage footballers might be completely the opposite way – to encourage them to relax. People need to be educated to relax. I'm like the rest of them now. I can't relax. It *must* be wrong. I've seen my doctor and he's suggested tranquilisers. I've refused them. I feel that would really be the end. But I need something.

"Managers don't worry that players can be totally destroyed by the time they're 30. They don't care when you're ill, if you're on the treatment table, or when you're in the reserves. You have to be a strong man to be a footballer. No wonder the weak go to the wall. Thank God it's a short life."

What makes it worse for Heighway, compared with the normal player, is that he has an alternative. When other footballers feel fed up, they have a simple compensation – but for football, so they keep saying, they'd be nobodies. Every footballer is child-like in his gratitude to the game.

"I'm always arguing with them about this. I tell them they owe football nothing."

His feelings have been heightened this season because the team hasn't had such a great start, not by Liverpool standards, but now they're hitting their best again.

"I sensed the crowd turning against us at Anfield, yet in over three seasons I've never lost at Anfield in a League match. The standards are so very high that you get the team sitting in the bath depressed after a 1–0 win."

Like most players, he thoroughly enjoyed schoolboy football, but: "As a player, I must be better equipped today. I am now an effective player, if your conception of an effective player is Liverpool's conception of an effective player. I don't feel overtrained, a stereotyped footballer. The manager does encourage us to express our individuality.

"I'm still learning because I'm a perfectionist. I *want* to win. The trouble is, I now think about it constantly, worry about it far too much."

He thinks that all footballers should be paid enough so that at 27, if they want to, they can retire from football, before the real humiliations begin. Heighway is 26 tomorrow. All afternoon, he'd talked as if his own retirement was imminent. Why doesn't he?

"I do look on this as a transitional stage. The best in my life is yet to come. That's what keeps me going. But at this moment I feel part of the team, loyal to the lads. I don't want to appear just a flash in the pan. And the highs, they're still as great as ever.

"When I cross-examine myself on all my motives – and I do so all the time – I think the main one is materialistic. It's the weakness of mankind. I now need the high wage to pay my high mortgage.

I don't want to become a teacher and have to struggle. I want to be a good teacher with no worries.

"I'm keener than ever to get into teaching. The longer I stay a footballer I realise that, I'll miss the lads and the competition but the day I pack it in I'll have an almighty sense of relief."

From *The Sunday Times*, 1973

World Club Championship Final, 1968

Arthur Hopcraft

Estudiantes de la Plata, in winning the World Club Championship, stayed faithful to the end to the antic gracelessness of the event. Their abrupt, offhand exit from London Airport on Thursday night, dismissing without hint of apology the matches arranged for this week against Arsenal and Birmingham, was an entirely appropriate finale: a collective gesture at England of the obscene kind that got Nobby Stiles ordered from the field in Buenos Aires.

The Argentinians' absence from Highbury tomorrow night and from St Andrews on Wednesday may be regarded as no great loss to football. The sourness, even pain, in the circumstances is that there is a distinct feeling of relief that the Argentinians have gone. Football loses all meaning when we reach the stage of being glad to call it off.

The recent history of the game as contested between Argentina and Britain is indeed distressingly ugly. Between the sending off of Rattin at Wembley in the 1966 World Cup and the simultaneous dismissals of George Best and Medina at Old Trafford on Wednesday night we have suffered Celtic's three gruesomely vengeful matches against Racing last year and then that spiteful first leg of this year's tie between Estudiantes and Manchester United in Buenos Aires. The game has never looked more nasty or more trivial.

Yet Sir Matt Busby, United's manager, is being honest to his professional nature when he shakes his grey head and smiles sadly, as he did at his press conference after Wednesday's return match, and insists that "you can't run away from these things".

Busby's view is the true competitor's: if the challenge exists it must be met. The fact that this particular event is really only a spectacle and not a logical competition is irrelevant to the committed contestant. It is at the moment the only World Cup Championship we have.

Wednesday's match, a 1–1 draw to give Estudiantes the title on aggregate of 2–1, was neither the brawl that some feared nor the uncomprehending collision of opposites that others promised. An English team lacking in organisation and individually short of form was cleverly, resolutely contained by a South American one thoroughly prepared for a specific exercise in defence and counter attack.

The difference was in method, not in moral basis. Certainly the Argentinians tackled with a ferocious abandon, the weight of the body following through behind the kick aimed roughly at the ball. Certainly they were well tutored in the techniques of irritation; arguing at every opportunity; intent on holding up the flow of the game. But none of that was being seen by the Old Trafford crowd for the first time: the Football League has several clubs with a talent for all of it.

The game was more of a bore than a disgrace. United, a goal behind within six minutes, never found enough pace, accuracy or invention to master this cynical, composed opposition.

The match rushed headlong into its double climax: Best's and Medina's sending off for fighting, with Medina being pushed and punched into submission by his own trainer, and then United's goal.

Later a group of Estudiantes players and officials arrived in the press room for no other reason, it seemed, than to give a brief, relished chanting of their club's and their country's names in the presence of men they believed had wickedly abused them. They grinned at us in proud rebuke.

By then both Busby and his team had conceded without hedging that the better side had won the title. But that admission did not end the bitterness created by the first match. Best, his lower lip purple and ridged, said the following day: "It's no good saying, 'Well, perhaps they weren't such a dirty side after all.' They *are* dirty. There's such a lot goes on that doesn't get noticed. Dave Sadler's gone off to the dentist this morning with two teeth hanging half out and his mouth all swollen up. He was punched. Who knew about that?"

Best was looking at the evening newspaper report of his banning from United's next two European Cup matches against Anderlecht, in punishment for his fight with Medina. He said he thought to be banned for one match would have been severe enough. Medina, he said, had elbowed him in the mouth as he walked past. "I just hit him back."

Medina, of course, in the well-drilled way of the Argentinians, went down as if he had been struck by a bus, just as Estudiantes' captain, and Best's marker, Malbernat, had done earlier when slapped by the Irishman.

This particular incident went unremarked by the referee, and Best would not talk about it. But I saw Malbernat stride five or six paces towards Best and spit in his face. Best's reply was delayed for two or three seconds. Malbernat stood facing him, as if waiting to be struck. When he was he fell elaborately.

It was plain enough that the Argentinians had the measure of Best's brittle irritability. Ironically, it was a night when they had no need to rile him. He played poorly, and afterwards said so without prevarication. "I never got going at all. It's been like that for two or three matches now. It was just bad that it had to happen for this big game."

Best's frank displeasure at himself can perhaps serve as the comment on this World Club Championship. The event needs time to change. It would be no kind of treatment to suppress it.

From The Observer, 1968

Bert Shakespeare: Fuhrer

Johnny Speight

Bert Shakespeare was a weedy little man with a shabby, ill fitting face that had once seen better days. His general physical appearance was like an old skinny potato that someone had struck matchsticks in for arms and legs. His clothes hung on him like loose skin, the dreary colours matching the fleshless complexion. He was one of nature's NCO's, an ex-sergeant major in the Pioneer Corps, a reject from the Police Training School and a failed prison warder. He was now a full-time football referee, and part-time scoutmaster. His power-hungry emaciated body yearned only for those despotic Saturday afternoons, when, with little black book, freshly sharpened pencil and gleaming chrome whistle clenched firmly between his plastic teeth, he could strut around on his matchstick legs feverishly taking names and sending players off.

As he practised the Nazi salute in front of the full-length mirror in his bedroom (his signal for a indirect free kick was like the funny little goose step he did when inspired by memories of Hitler) he thought wistfully how much he would have liked to take his cane on the pitch with him. . . .

AH YES, A FEW SHARP SLASHES ROUND THEIR LEGS AND THAT'D STOP THE SWEARING, BUT THEY WOULDN'T LET HIM USE THAT. NEVER MIND, GETTING A STAR PLAYER SUSPENDED COULD BE JOY ENOUGH.

Bert Shakespeare disliked footballers. He had good reason for this. It was much easier to dislike a thing you hated, and if there was anything he hated more than footballers it was football fans, and he disliked them too. If he was allowed his way he wouldn't suspend only the players, he'd suspend the fans as well. He had good reason for this too. He had good reason for everything. Besides, their language was bad. Worse than some of the players.

And if there was one thing he hated worse than football players, it was lad language. He never used it himself except in private to his wife. And if there was one thing he hated worse than football players, it was his wife. He would suspend her, too, if he could.

"A two-week suspension would do her good," he remarked.

"I beg your pardon?"

125

He looked up at the fat woman; they were the only two on the bus.

"I was referring to my wife," he said.

"Oh, you're married then?" She couldn't keep the disappointment off her kindly fat face. Some very thin people are fatally attracted to some very fat people and vice versa, and she knew this – or thought she knew it. Knowledge had never really interested her, but she supposed she was entitled to think it if she wanted.

I'd like to have charge of the buses, he thought. I wouldn't allow fat people on them for a start. They take up too much room for one thing, especially fat coloured people. He didn't quite know why he thought fat coloured people took up more room on buses than fat white people, especially if they were the same size. But like the fat woman, he supposed he was entitled to think this if he wanted to. The fact that she really didn't think this was nothing to do with it.

Thoughts like this and many others passed through his mind as he made his way to the match. . . .

If didn't bother him if the Football Association was a front for the Communist Party. He'd overheard the remark in a pub. But it didn't concern him. He'd make a good commissar. He knew that. He might make a bad husband, or a bad thin man, or a bad fat man if he'd been a fat man, or a bad football referee, but he wouldn't make a bad commissar. He'd make a bloody good one, there was no doubt about that.

He sat playing with his whistle and flicking his upper denture out on the end of his tongue and back again with a sharp click – a habit of his when deep in thought. His thoughts weren't very deep, but he was deep in them. So deep that he was completely unconscious of what he was doing – a natural state for him.

The fat woman sat and watched him. He's got nice teeth she thought. They were better than her own. Her own were only National Health teeth, but his were private teeth. That was easy to see. You don't get teeth like that on the National Health, she thought. For all she knew, hers may not have been National Health teeth, anyway she'd bought them second-hand in the Portobello Road, with no history attached, so they could quite easily have been upper-class teeth, or even aristocratic teeth for all she knew, but she supposed they were only working-class teeth. In fact, she would have felt very ill at ease if she thought she was wearing teeth above her station.

Bert Shakespeare's teeth had played a very dramatic part in league football. Not the new private teeth he wore now, but the old National Health teeth which had been very loose. The trouble was his mouth had shrunk far beyond the ratio allowed for normal shrinkage and if his mouth was opened suddenly, or his head turned too swiftly, the teeth were inclined to shoot out. Many minutes of injury time played were the result of his having to halt the game while he retrieved his teeth.

On one notable occasion he had turned his head quickly to rebuke a player for an infringement and his teeth had shot out and inflicted a nasty gash over the left eye of an international inside-forward and before he could retrieve his teeth another player's boot had crushed them to small pieces on the frosty ground. Shakespeare was so annoyed he sent both teams off and cancelled the game.

They're getting a lot of natives on these buses, he thought as the conductor approached him. This one seemed all right though. He seemed to know where the bus was going. But he preferred the white ones himself. With black conductors he always tried to avoid touching their hands as they gave him his ticket. He always had the right money as well. He didn't want money they had handled in his pocket.

The bus was nearing the ground now. They seemed to be getting a few more black players as well these days. He didn't like them either. He'd been forced to send one of them off a few weeks back. He hadn't done anything. It was just that Bert couldn't stand the sight of him mixing with the other white players. He told the F.A. the blackie swore at him. They've got to take my word, he thought. He was the ref. His word was law.

He wondered if there'd be a bottle of scotch in his room today. A lot of clubs put a bottle of scotch in the referee's room on a cold day. Mustn't drink too much before the game though, he thought. He'd done it once. Well, he'd been depressed and he'd drunk a bit more than was good for him before he'd gone onto the pitch. He wasn't drunk but he'd found it a bit hard to keep up with the game.

This was the stop. He got off the bus and mingled with the crowds. Early as it was, there were thousands going in. Uncouth louts most of them. The only football fans Bert had time for were the wealthy club directors. He didn't mind those – especially if they left a bottle of scotch in his room. Bert couldn't be bribed. But any home side that put a bottle of scotch in his room got all the luck that was going.

Bert scowled as he entered his room. No scotch today. Mean swines.

He shivered as he strode out onto the cold November pitch. I could have done with that scotch today, he thought. They were bloody daft not to give it to him. An oversight like that could easily cost them two very valuable points. Bloody fools, he thought. To risk chucking away two championship points for the price of a bottle of scotch.

From the *Johnny Haynes Testimonial Programme*, 1968

Bridging The Gap

Willis Hall

I have sat in on many a rousing argument, at every level from television studio to saloon bar bog, about why nobody has succeeded in making a cracking good film with a soccer theme. Indeed, apart from Sydney Howard in *Up For The Cup*, a comic epic made way back in 1933, the subject seems to have been left well alone. (Keen moviegoers will not need telling that the film titled *Arsenal*, made in the U.S.S.R. in 1929 concerns the workers' revolution and has nothing at all to do with the well-known football club that shares the same name.)

And yet soccer, with its world-wide following, would seem ripe for transition to the big screen.

As I say, I have listened to pundits on both sides of the fence, to film makers and to soccer theorists, and the arguments they have put forward have been informed and innumerable. I have, in fact, stuck in my own intelligent oar a time or two. But nobody has ever seemed to come up with a satisfactory answer to the problem.

Nobody, at least, until I chatted to Jackie Charlton not long ago. And the solution is so obvious and so simple that I have been kicking myself ever since.

"The fact is," said Big Jack, "that actors haven't got footballers legs."

He's dead right. They haven't. Not by any stretch of the imagination.

And even if they had, how in God's good name would one set about casting them? Like they did it in those Alice Faye type pictures in the forties? You know the ones I mean, where this leering film director lines up a dozen or so glamorous cuties and invites them to hitch up their skirts. Modestly, for his and our benefit, the young ladies flash their calves.

You could never invite actors to behave like that – it would look more like a weeding-out heat for a knobbly knees contest at a third-rate holiday camp.

Not, mark you, that I'm suggesting that there is anything

physically *wrong* with actors' legs. Perish the thought. On the contrary, generally speaking, they are mostly more than functional – put to the use for which they were intended.

Decked out in tights, hovering below a cod-piece, and strutting across the boards at Stratford or for dodging about on in a duel scene at the National Theatre, most actors' legs have never been known to fail to please. But stick them in Umbro stockings and Adidas boots and ask them to show their paces on well-cut turf and all at once the faults begin to show through.

And I speak as one who knows, for it's been my unhappy experience to ask actors to portray footballers in more than one dramatic piece for television.

Finding actors who *think* they can imitate footballers is not difficult. Most actors are pretty sure in their own minds that they can imitate anyone, given half a chance. And ring up any actor's agent about his client's proficiency on the football park and a close approximation of the following conversation will result:

"Archie? Play football? You're not serious, are you?"

"I'm in deadly earnest. You see, I'm casting a play about a footballer and –––––"

"Archie was playing striker for his Middlesborough Junior Stage School when he was *10 years old*!"

"Really, I didn't know ––––––"

"But I'm telling you, dear boy. When Archie was with the Bursley Repertory Theatre, he not only skippered the Rep 11, he also played 160 games of senior amateur football in the Central League."

"If he'd like to pop along we're auditioning at –––––"

"Of course, you know about his trial for Chelsea?"

"To be absolutely honest, I ––––––"

"They wanted him to turn pro. I had hell's own job getting Dave Sexton to leave this office with his contract unsigned."

"He sounds like just the sort of chap we're ––––––"

"And Arsenal. They were after him. Bertie Mee was an embarrassment, down on his bended knees. I could have done a swap. If Archie had gone to Arsenal, I could have had Charlie George and Peter Storey in the touring production of *No, No, Nanette*!"

And so forth, and so forth.

Making allowances and taking the agent's eulogies with a sack of salt, you would still be excused for forming the opinion that his client was possessed of *some* slight idea of the principles of football.

Not a bit of it.

When Archie turns up for the audition (along with a dozen or so other budding Thespian Bobby Moores), you will quickly discover that his interest in the sport is rather less than cursory. It's just possible that he might have attended a matinee performance of *Zigger-Zagger* – if not, and taxed about his knowledge of the game, he'll probably reply: "Soccer? Ah! Mmmm! Yes! Now just let me think – is that the one with the round ball or the sausage shaped thingy?"

Coupled with which, and as Jackie Charlton astutely observed, he won't have footballers' legs.

What he will bring to the part, however, is unbounded enthusiasm. All actors are brimful of it. Enthusiasm is part and parcel of every actor's stock-in-trade.

There was one television play that I wrote when, on the first day of rehearsal, you never saw 11 more enthusiastic lads gathered together. Even the director was infected by their enthusiasm.

"They may not look much like footballers," he said. "But they *are* enthusiastic. Give them a couple of weeks and you'll think they're Leeds United."

I had some slight reservations but I was willing to go along with him.

After a week of rehearsals, those boys were so keyed up you might easily have mistaken the atmosphere in that rehearsal room for that of a Wembley dressing room on Cup Final day.

Some few days before we were due to record the play, the director organised a real game for them in order to keep them at their peak. There were a lot of football plays about at the time and it was easy enough to find our lads some opposition from the ranks of their colleagues.

And so it came about that, at 10.30 on a bleak out-of-season Wednesday morning, 11 pretend-footballers were ushered into a *real* dressing-room prior to taking part in a *real* football match, some of them for the first time in their lives.

The dressing-room contained *real* showers, and our lads were provided with a *real* football strip and *real* boots by the television props department, who had further excelled themselves by bringing along *real* oranges for refreshment at half-time. There was even *real* liniment for the lads to rub on their limbs.

The footballing actors chattered excitedly and enthusiastically as they prepared themselves. In no time at all they had mastered the intricacies of tie-ups and laces and were dressed and ready for the battle ahead. It had to be admitted that they looked the part – viewed above the waist.

I had myself invited an ex-professional player along to act as

131

referee, as well as have a good laugh, and it was his whistle that summoned both teams out onto the park.

It was at this point that Life and Art failed to fuse.

Directly outside the dressing-rooms was a concrete path, no more than three feet wide, but it was a hazard that had to be crossed in order to get onto the actual pitch.

Twenty-one actor-footballers managed to get across safely. One actor-footballer did not.

The casualty was a chap in his thirties. He had never played football in his life. He had never before worn football boots. He was unused to football studs.

As he ran out of the dressing-room he stamped one studded boot on the concrete and up he went, one leg first and then the other, propelled into a full somersault from which he landed, inelegantly, chin first, on the concrete path.

We lifted him gently and carried him back into the dressing-room. We laid him on a bench.

If the *Guinness Book of Records* is interested, I would put him forward as the only man ever to be injured at football who has never actually kicked a ball.

He was taken to hospital, his chin was stitched, and he was returned to us in time to play his part in the television studio.

As for the actual game we played, and for the record books, our side of pretend-footballers beat the other side of pretend-footballers by the odd goal in three, though we played with a man short.

It was not a memorable match.

The players hadn't got footballers' legs.

Believe me, I am not knocking the acting profession. After all, I'm sure they did as well as, if not better than, say, Charlie George and Peter Storey would do in the touring production of *No, No, Nanette!*

From *Sportsworld*, 1973

Hard Man, Soft Centre

Julie Welch

After a particularly austere tackle, Norman Hunter will extricate himself with a fast backward foxtrot, hands raised as though about to be frisked and bestowing on all and sundry a grin the size of Marble Arch.

The grin is a mixture of the rueful and the conciliatory. It spends most of the game fixed to his face, and when he trains it is still present, a dogged, enthusiastic generous grin that the toughest exertion seems unable to obliterate.

Off the field, the grin is somewhat doused. Hunter's features are gently funereal; eyes a murky blue–brown, long nose and extensive sidewhiskering. Only the jaw is ominous; it juts out determinedly and looks as though it cuts glass in its spare time.

Mention to him his reputation as a hard man, and he takes on the glazed look of a breakfast kipper. Everyone, he says, asks him that. "It doesn't mean anything to me. My job is to win the ball and give it to a better player. I don't sit and plot about it. It's just something I accept.

"You see a player with the ball, and you think, *well*. . . . You go hard for it, and if you come out with it, you come out with it. If you thought about it you'd never do it, would you?

"I don't mind my image. Now Leeds are starting to get recognised, and the collective hard tag will die gradually. But I've still got to play the same way. It takes all types to make a team. If I don't win the ball, I'm not doing my job. If I started knocking it down, putting it around in the box, pretending I was a good player – well, we'd get into trouble.

"It would only hurt me if anyone down here criticised me. Outside people don't worry me. Coming back from an away trip, the lads sit and talk, and sometimes I get teased. Phew, bad player you are, they say. I used to get upset, but now I laugh at it."

The flintier aspects of Hunter's game are legend. Faced with an oncoming attacker, he bristles with the delighted indignation of a mongrel dog sighting a postman. His utter enjoyment of a game, his rejection of possible defeat and his constant uproarious energy

"Hello, Desmond, lad . . . things not so good?"

have been vital to Leeds in the past and show every sign of waking the England team out of its somnabulance.

Against Austria at Wembley, a few playful butts from behind were all that was needed of his defensive repertoire. Freed from being a one-man ambush, his attacking qualities were obvious. Advancing with his dog-paddling run, he was instrumental in the two best English goals, combining hearteningly with Tony Currie.

"I like to come forward. You get a little bit bored of defending. At Wembley we had an awful lot of room; no pressure. If it's 0–0 and someone's harassing you, it's harder. I found it very easy to play with Roy McFarland. I don't know why, but I can talk to him. You've got to chat to each other, you see.

"But I've no illusions about my game. I'm fortunate – I've played in a good team. You're bound to get better. I do. I always improve. I'm not basically fast, not fast enough. I haven't got natural speed, not like Madeley or Reaney – McQueen. He's 6 ft 3 in, and he can fly."

For a man who sometimes does not tackle opponents so much as break them down for resale as scrap, Hunter is an astonishingly amiable man. Speak of him in Leeds, and a shower of anecdotes will be invoked about his friendliness, his generosity, his involvement with charity work.

He trains as willingly and as fiercely as he plays; afterwards, enthusiasm abated, he pads around in socks, clutching a large tub of baby powder and curtained in baggy track suit, like a statue about to be unveiled.

"I'm two different people on and off. I don't know why it should be. You've got to win, you see; that's what keeps you going. You've *got* to. You can't say, well, we won that last year, we'll take it easy this.

"I'm fairly quick tempered, but it's up and down and gone. No grudges. Just for two seconds I really go. The silliest thing I ever did was to go after that fellow Rivera in the Cup Winners' Cup at Salonika

"He kicked me and I went after him. If he'd been closer, I'd have hit him, but he'd walked away. By the time I'd trudged all that distance, my temper had gone down again and I didn't want to do anything, I just laid my hands on him and I got sent off.

"It was a bit emotional, walking down the tunnel. We'd lost to Sunderland, we were trying to win something back, we'd played so well and then I had to get sent off. It was a long tunnel. I'd only got halfway when the final whistle went. We deserved to hammer them, and it was all over and I was in that tunnel, and we'd lost.

"When I lose I've got to talk about it. Some keep it inside them. I go home and relive it with the wife. She just nods and says yes or no.

"Sometimes I'm close to tears. I'm emotional you see. Football makes me emotional. Not many people can explain what it's like when you play all season and you get to Wembley or somewhere, and at the end you and the lads walk down the tunnel while the other lot are doing the lap of honour."

From *The Observer*, 1973

A Village Goalkeeper

Arthur Hopcraft

We were joined sometimes by a sad, uncommon figure of rickety assemblage and haphazard speech, called Vic. His age was indeterminable, and a subject of recurrent speculation. He was a kind of village indulgence or communal responsibility. He was special because it was impossible to categorise him except as himself.

He was not lunatic, although he could barely read or count or frame a dozen consecutive words to make a spoken sentence. He was not a cripple in the sense of immobility, although he could not co-ordinate the movements of his limbs with enough certainty to go to work. He was seen in public houses, so was not a child; but he kept school hours in the daytime, emerging from his house when we were free for play, and out and about all day long when we were on holiday. He was treated as a child by children and as an adult by adults. He was ugly and disjointed and he stammered and spat; yet there was quickly recognisable in him an intention of gentleness struggling to work its way through the brutish surface and the built-in tangle of communication equipment that frustrated him. This tenderness was visible in his face, which would lose its twist and let the helplessness in the eyes make the point when the tongue could not overcome its knots. He looked more of a man, more deserving of civility then than at any other time. Not even the most pampered, most timid of the local children was ever frightened by poor, preposterous Vic.

His passion for football brought him dramatic, alarming collisions. He would come lurching and capering into our games, knees collapsing and scissoring beyond management, elbows flicking and fingers jerking up and down, left and right, as he fought in his own way to maintain a precarious verticality with the ground. "I's in -g-g-goal," he would shout, heading for the place of glamour where he could imagine his possession of easy agility and faultless timing. This was very touching: the tortured angularity, the blundering dizzy movements, the face clamped in earnestness, and his bellowing monosyllables of rage and frustration as he missed the ball and crashed in a heap on the mud. He made a noise like a spilled box of dominoes when the ground was hard. But he would struggle upright, spitting and gurgling, teetering backwards on his heels, thrusting his long white jaw up in front and his long cheese-wire fingers down behind in another of his unique acts of balance. Someone hit him hard in the face from close in on one occasion, when we had a real football with a leather casing and an inexpertly tied leather lace sealing the aperture. The lace bit into his skin, slashing one of his eyebrows, and there was a spurt of blood. We hesitated, "S-s-s'all right," he shouted, brushing the blood away with a thumb and bringing another little gush; and he aimed a kick at the ball, missed, spun round twice in a flailing of arms as if overbalancing in a rowing boat, and settled in an absurd imitation of a goalkeeper's crouch, the thin head wagging and shaking spots of blood on to his knees. He looked heroic.

He was totally inept at football. His unpredictable movements influenced the game in a furious lucky-dip way; the ball struck him often. If he managed to catch it in both hands that tautly misshapen face would relax into a little boy's beam of wonder. If he socked the ball with his fist he would hee-haw in triumph.

There were times when his incapacities were misread by people not familiar with him; when someone would make a hasty assumption of imbecility or abjection and, trying to impress the rest of us, would play the tormentor. I watched one of these incidents with a rancid fascination. The interloper was red-haired and tubby and he had a sprig of elder which he kept jabbing into Vic's face, tickling and yapping. Vic made his clumsy brushing-away movements with his hands, struggling to speak, the splayed fingers missing the twig and scraping his nose and chin, and the red-haired boy laughed in delight at this bonus. Vic's face screwed up into a look of deepest bewilderment, and then abruptly changed into the normal features of an irritated adult, as his emotions overpowered his physical and nervous defects and blazed a path through the shame and humility which usually obscured other feelings. He stumbled forward, threw out those crusty hinged arms and clasped them shut, and the red-haired boy found himself in a metallic, rattling embrace, which must have felt like being held between two rows of clucking false teeth. Vic was mouthing some unintelligible impressions: "I's g-g-gun-gun-gunna-ger-gun-gun. . . ." the red-haired boy was squealing and sobbing in terror.

We watched callously. Vic squeezed those sharp-edged arms, his wrists crossed and his hands going like a pair of pecking birds. When he unravelled himself, stumbling and still keeping hold of his captive for balance, first with one hand and then with the other, he was gasping from his stomach. The red-haired boy, released at last, was white and blank in the face like a pudding cloth across a basin. Then great sobs welled up from round his braces and came bubbling through his lips, and he went back home with a disgraceful secret to hide about the day he went bear-baiting and the beast broke loose.

But poor Vic was broken by a trickier, deeper-plunging intrusion into his grevious privacy. My group heard about it in troubling, piecemeal snatches; overheard about it, more accurately. Some working youths, turning idleness into elaborate cunning, pondered on his sexual interest and capability and decided to try him out. That Beryl, they said to him, the tall one with the glasses and the red nose, she was sweet on him; she was easy, as well, they told him. He was a man, wasn't he? She was eating her heart out for him, they said; but he'd have to push himself a bit. Go on, Vic, they told him. Why didn't he wait in the entry for her? When it got dark? She went for fish and chips on Thursdays, half past eight about. He was a man, wasn't he?

So it seems that Vic took up his position in the gloom of the entry half-way along the terrace row, with a collar and a tie like a prune-stone under his left ear, and his boots polished. And the gaunt Beryl came clattering down the alley in her wedge-soled shoes, was suddenly set upon by this jabbering shuffling rapist smelling of coal-shed and dog-lust, and she screamed and hit out, and Vic grabbed and gabbled, and they fell down, and Vic's trouser buttons were undone as always, and the watching youths ran off as people arrived and sent for the policeman.

"Well, I knew summat like that ud 'appen woon o' these nights," old women said in the bread queue.

"Yo cor trust 'em, these dafties."

"They should put 'im away somewheer."

"Its's the devil rising-gup in 'im, Missis."

Vic was not put away, but he had to go to court, where Beryl told her story of outrage and the policeman explained how hard it was to gather a coherent explanation from the defendant, but that he appeared to be implicating some other persons who were not present.

Vic returned to us, morose and enfeebled. He sat on the bank like a dead bonfire and watched us play football, but he never went in goal again.

From *The Great Apple Raid*, 1970

Away Games

Harold Pinter

GUS: What town are we in? I've forgotten.

BEN: I've told you. Birmingham.

GUS: Go on! *(He looks with interest about the room.)* That's in the Midlands. The second biggest city in Great Britain. I'd never have guessed. *(He snaps his fingers.)* Eh, it's Friday today, isn't it? It'll be Saturday tomorrow.

BEN: What about it?

GUS: (excited): We could go and watch the Villa.

BEN: They're playing away.

GUS: No, are they? Caarr! What a pity.

BEN: Anyway, there's no time. We've got to get straight back.

GUS: Well, we have done in the past, haven't we? Stayed over and watched a game, haven't we? For a bit of relaxation.

BEN: Things have tightened up, mate. They've tightened up.

(GUS chuckles to himself.)

GUS: I saw the Villa get beat in a cup tie once. Who was it against now? White shirts. It was one-all at half time. I'll never forget it. Their opponents won by a penalty. Talk about drama. Yes, it was a disputed penalty. Disputed. They got beat two-one, anyway, because of it. You were there yourself.

BEN: Not me.

GUS: Yes, you were there. Don't you remember that disputed penalty?

BEN: No.

GUS: He went down just inside the area. Then they said he was just acting. I didn't think the other bloke touched him myself. But the referee had the ball on the spot.

BEN: Didn't touch him! What are you talking about? He laid him out flat!

GUS: Not the Villa. The Villa don't play that sort of game.

BEN: Get out of it.

(Pause.)

GUS: Eh, that must have been here, in Birmingham.

BEN: What must?

GUS: The Villa. That must have been here.

BEN: They were playing away.

139

GUS: Because you know who the other team was? It was the Spurs. It was Tottenham Hotspur.

BEN: Well, what about it?

GUS: We've never done a job in Tottenham.

BEN: How do you know?

GUS: I'd remember Tottenham.

(BEN turns on his bed to look at him.)

BEN: Don't make me laugh, will you?

(BEN turns back and reads. GUS yawns and speaks through his yawn.)

GUS: When's he going to get in touch? *(Pause.)* Yes, I'd like to see another football match. I've always been an ardent football fan. Here, what about coming to see the Spurs tomorrow?

BEN: (tonelessly): They're playing away.

GUS: Who are?

BEN: The Spurs.

GUS: Then they might be playing here.

BEN: Don't be silly.

GUS: If they're playing away they might be playing here. They might be playing the Villa.

BEN: (tonelessly): But the Villa are playing away.

(Pause. An envelope slides under the door, right. GUS sees it. He stands, looking at it.)

BEN: Away. They're all playing away.

From *The Dumb Waiter*, 1960

Cup Final, 2072

Jack Rosenthal

Next Saturday, London United and Arts' Council-sponsored New Accrington Stanley will grace the polyester-fibre turf of Wembley for the 200th F.A. Cup Final.

Already the match is a sell-out. A capacity crowd of 27 is expected in the Sentimental Spectators' Enclosure – over and above the 988 million who'll be watching on TV, both on earth and in the Stretford End Penal Colony on the moon.

Unfortunately, the TV audience won't include several million viewers in Asia, engrossed in their own transmission of the vital bottom-of-the-table struggle between Crystal Palace and Peking Albion, now managed by veteran Tommy Docherty. (Until Wednesday, when he joins Antarctic Thistle until Friday.)

But, for the rest of us, Wembley promises perhaps the purest exhibition of football skill since the Peter Storey Prize for Gentlemanly Behaviour was introduced in the late 1970s.

A quick glance at the teams shows us why.

London United will be skippered by the only white player in the team, George Eastham – believed by pundits to be now actually playing his last season. Or possibly his last-but-one. Or two.

Seven members of the team are Honours Graduates in Tactics, European Slang, Latin-American Petulance and Post-Goal Self-Control.

And two of them – Zap Best (grandson of a former Miss Sweden) and Pow Best (grandson of a former Panamanian fashion model) – are Emeritus Professors in Body Checknology at Cold Blow Lane University.

New Accrington Stanley, apart from the balding but beautiful Charlton Sisters in midfield, have six male internationals – including Zip Best (grandson of a former Italian actress), Turk Best (grandson of a former Hawaiin air-hostess) and Arnold Best (grandson of an unknown Oldham usherette who, in her youth, unthinkingly had one night out in Manchester and two Babychams too many).

In the pre-match cabaret, the spotlight once again falls on the Super Leeds Corps de Ballet (runners-up 108 times in the last 108 years in the Formation Dance Team Competition) under its ageing but perservering choreographer, Sir Don Revie.

The Cup itself will be presented by Princess Victoria (apparently not the grand-daughter of George Best) probably on horseback.

She will also present the coveted David Coleman Award to the first TV commentator who burbles "And that's what it's all about" every time a player kicks the ball.

Now who's going to win?

Speculation plummeted to fever-pitch this morning, when both managers – trained at the Alf Ramsey School of Communications – actually opened their mouths slightly, then quickly closed them again.

We wish both sides good programming in their play on Saturday, with lots of automatic Hopeful Centres, and no ugly incidents like beating a man or shooting.

In the quaint words of an ancient saying lost from the language ever since the 1950's – "The game's the thing, and may the best team win."

From *The Evening Standard 1972 Cup Final Issue*

Oh, No, Not Him Again

Hunter Davies

Brian Clough got into his silver Mercedes and drove himself home for lunch, still wearing the green nylon shirt and felt carpet slippers he'd been wearing all morning while he'd been watching his players training.

Football managers don't usually go in for leisurely lunches with their wives and families. Football managers usually eat football for lunch. As football managers go, Mr Clough is very strange. He has time for life other than football. As for the juxtaposition of the flash car and the unflash clothes, that's not really so strange, though his players think it's funny, even eccentric. Mr Clough is a mass of contradictions. In public, especially on TV, he's the man the country's football fans love to hate, the loud-mouth, the know-all. In private, well, the testimonies to his softness and kindness and humanity are almost embarrassing.

Back at Derby County F.C.'s ground, home of the present Champions of the Football League, a gaggle of local journalists were sitting in a room outside the shrine, patiently waiting for Cloughy to come back from his lunch and give them an audience.

"I cover about 10 League clubs in the Midlands," said one free-lance journalist. "Every Friday we call them and all we usually get is a list of 12 names. But with Cloughy, he always gives you a story. In the five years since he came to Derby, I can't tell you how much my salary's gone up every year. Just because of him. He's a genius."

The hours went by. Mr Clough returned and padded in from time to time, supplying food and drink, saying a player wanted to see him, or his chairman was waiting, he wouldn't be long. Nobody was at all worried.

"I know I'll get some copy in the end," said another journalist. "He's murder to get on the phone and he's usually late for an appointment, but even London journalists, if they're prepared to come up and hang around, get something from him."

Mr Clough's office is large and spacious with an enormous bar

143

running across one side. He eventually had all the journalists lined up on one side, drinks in their willing hands, while he padded up and down, rampaging against his enemies, answering questions and shouting obscenities at a TV set which was blaring away in a corner. "That's your opinion," he kept on shouting when a TV sports expert on the box was giving his predictions. One thing people with strong opinions can't stand is people with strong opinions.

"I don't regard winning the League as Utopia, though we still haven't had the credit we deserved for doing it. We did it with no gimmicks, unlike Leeds, and with the smallest pool of players in the Division. Whichever teams win the Championship in the next 20 years, and I hope teams like Rochdale and Halifax will be amongst them, none of them will have as hard a job as we had. We did it with 12 players. Those London bums can't explain it. All right, I admit we did it against the odds, but we did it with ability. Revie has been going crackers trying to explain it ever since. I give Allison and Shankly their due. They both said we could do it. But it's those bums on the Fleet Street sports pages I hate most. They called it a fluke. They wrote us off months before the season ended. They're so biased in favour of the London clubs it's revolting. Then when we did win, they weren't big enough or competent enough to get round it. They just ignored us.

"When I'm proved wrong, I'm big enough and competent enough to get round it. If I tell my lads they'll hammer Arsenal 2–0 and we don't, I'll think of some explanations, I'll find some reasons. I'll face up to it. But not those London bums. Right, last drinks. I've got my bairn's birthday party at four o'clock. You've got two more minutes."

Brian Clough has had all sorts and conditions of bums to rail against, right throughout his life. He's always been the underdog, the one overlooked or under-rated, the one who's been told to shut up and don't be so aggressive, who do you think you are. There's no doubt he's thrived on it. This season, for the first time in his life, he's *expected* to do well. Naturally, his rivals have been gloating over some of his team's rather surprising defeats. Is he up to success?

In the car home he agreed that having people against him, having had things hard as a player, had been a spur, but at the same time he'd been made very unhappy. "People talk about my career. What a bloody joke. I never had a career."

He was born in Middlesbrough in 1936, one of six brothers and two sisters. His father used to work in a sweet factory. He went to

144

the local secondary modern school, where he was no good academically and cared only about football, cricket and tennis. But he wasn't really much good at them either; he never thought about being a footballer. At 15 he went into the offices of the local megalith – ICI – and worked for more than two years as a junior clerk in the Work Study department. Right from the first day he started lashing out at authority, though with little success.

"I was told that my clocking-in time would be 12 minutes past seven every morning. Twelve minutes past seven! Can you think of a bloody sillier time? I wanted to know which genius had thought up that, but they wouldn't tell me. How ICI has survived all these years by starting people at 12 minutes past seven I'll never know."

He was playing park football at weekends. When he was about 17, Middlesbrough took him on as a part-timer, though with no promises of making him a professional. Soon after, he was called up for national service.

"That's when I came to my senses, from 18 to 20 in the Forces. I thought hell's teeth, what am I going to do with life? I'm not going back to ICI. So I wrote to Middlesbrough instead. I had to ask them to take me on as a professional. They didn't ask me."

After six months in Middlesbrough's reserves, on £7 a week, he asked to go. "I told them they were treating me unfairly. I said give us me cards, I'm going. They gave me a rise." He got a few first team games, then he dropped back into the reserves, feeling he was a failure.

"I was only the fourth choice for centre-forward. No-one was telling me I could make it, so I was very depressed. At 21 you need your confidence boosted. At 25 you can strut around and look after yourself. The only person who convinced me I was any good was Peter Taylor, the first team goalie. He was the first person to tell me I was bloody good. He said that in another set-up I could do really well. But the buggers wouldn't let me go. As a reserve they wouldn't transfer me, then when I made the first team they wouldn't let me go either. I don't know why."

When he finally made the first team, his success was phenomenal. He was the prototype cannonball centre-forward, straight out of the boys' comics, who threw himself at every chance and scored goals like clockwork. He set up a goal-scoring record which still stands, scoring 251 goals in 271 League matches. No footballer since the war has scored goals so quickly or so consistently or at such a young age as Brian Clough. (Dixie Dean in the Thirties is the only one who can match his record.) But by doing it all in Second Division matches he didn't get the national coverage and credit he was convinced he deserved. Eventually his goal-scoring ability did get him into the England team, but he got only two full caps in all. "It was rank bad selection on the part of the England committee."

Despite all his goals, he spent every season at Middlesbrough asking for a transfer, hoping to go to a First Division side, so he could really show them. Middlesbrough made him captain hoping to keep him quiet, but this led to further trouble. A group of the players signed a round-robin, asking for him to be relieved of the captaincy. "I don't know why they did it. All I know is there were a few scoundrels around at the time. I was very hurt. I took being captain very seriously." He remained captain, but he was no happier. "The only thing I enjoyed during my six years at Middlesbrough was scoring goals. From Saturday to Saturday I was very unhappy. My ability was never utilised, by me or the management. Only goals kept me sane. That was the only pleasure."

At last, in 1961, he was transferred to Sunderland for £45,000. They were also in the Second Division, but two seasons later they were promoted to the First – without Clough's help. On Boxing Day 1962, in a match against Bury, he injured his knee, an injury which finished his career. He was only 26. The injury dragged on for a further 18 months, as he tried to make a come-back – he did return for three First Division games – but he eventually had to pack in playing. He helped on the coaching side for a bit at Sunderland and then was out of work for a while till Hartlepool took him on as manager in 1965, at the age of 29, making him the youngest manager in the country.

At Hartlepool he drove the team coach, went round the working men's clubs with cap in hand to get money to pay the players, and offered to go without his own salary to keep the club solvent. Nevertheless, he faced every issue head on, ducking no decisions. "I didn't know up to then that I could be a manager, but I learned very quickly. The biggest crime a player can commit is giving the ball away. The biggest crime for a manager is copping out of his word. I warned four players about their conduct. It didn't improve, so I said out, to all four of them. It left me with only seven players, but if a manager threatens something, he's got to keep his word."

At Hartlepool he had as his assistant Peter Taylor, the same Peter Taylor who was his friend at Middlesbrough. Today, he's his assistant manager at Derby. Inside football it's known that Taylor has made an important contribution to Clough and to

Derby, though the general public never hears about him. He's a perfect counterpoint to Clough – quiet, retiring, with no desire to hear himself talk or be talked about. But in many ways, despite the public image, Clough is not the hard man of Derby. It's Taylor who's the toughie.

In five years they've transformed Derby, taking them from the foot of the Second Division to the top of Division One, doubling the gates, revitalising the club and the team. It's noticeable how many Derby directors have gone since Clough arrived, though the chairman, Sam Longson, who made the brave and inspired decision to bring him from Hartlepool, is still there and even carries a pin-up picture of Clough in his wallet.

There have been stories about Clough going to other, bigger and more glamorous clubs, or even taking over the England team, but he seems content at Derby. In November he signed a new five-year contract. Despite a poor start in the League, Derby have managed to gird their loins and get themselves together and find enough form and spirit to beat Benfica in the European Cup. This means they're the last British team left in the competition (the next match will be in March) as Glasgow Celtic have been knocked out.

For a small club, they've reimbursed him well. Last season he must have made almost £20,000 with all the bonuses.

What a manager does to a team is abstract. You can't categorise it. It's a matter of inspiration. Most of his present stars came from lowly clubs, overlooked by other managers. He got McFarland, for example, now England's centre half, from Tranmere for £24,000. He also managed to coax that extra bit out of elderly stars like Dave Mackay, whom Spurs thought had had his day when they let him go for £4,000. Now, with success, he's in the money and can buy made stars like £170,000 Colin Todd and £250,000 David Nish.

He has a passion for players of the right character, which all managers have, and he's willing to bawl out any shirkers in public, to humiliate them, to grind the skivers or phonies or cowards or cheats into the ground, whether it is players or journalists. (He has his acolytes now, but over the years quite a few journalists have been told they weren't wanted at his club.)

Because people are amazed, even frightened, by his honesty, he's always believed. Because he is always willing to praise, his players feel that if he says they can do it, they really can. He tells them all the time how he envies them. He'd give up his large salary as manager if he could be out there playing with them.

"I haven't found a compensation yet for scoring goals. I fed on goals. They were ecstasy to me. It was like a bloody drug. But scoring the quickest 250 goals in history wasn't enough. I never got to Wembley. I never won a Championship. I would love to have been one of Derby's 12 who did it last year. Playing is the biggest pleasure."

There were shouts of delight as he arrived home in his Mercedes. He was slightly late for the party, but they were all waiting for him, 16 eight-year-old boys. The party was for Simon, his eldest. He has another son, Nigel, six, and a daughter Elizabeth, who is five. He went in, clapped his hands and told them to get ready. He has had 14 kids in his Mercedes, but he decided 16 was too many, so they all set off down the suburban street, running behind him, shouting: "We are the Champions." We got to a park and he arranged two sides and started them playing. He was to be the referee, though Elizabeth was to stay beside him and do the actual whistle-blowing.

An onlooker could easily have thought he was slightly deranged. He wasn't running a children's party game between two sets of eight-year-olds. It was deadly serious. He treated the kids as real professional footballers, which of course they responded to. He padded up and down in his carpet slippers, screaming out instructions, like that school-master in the football match in *Kes* who was convinced he was running Manchester United.

"Do that once more, Si, and you're off!" he shouted at his eight-year-old-son. "Who said you could pick that ball up? The whistle didn't blow for a throw-in, did it? No it did not. Handball!"

He let them get away with nothing, not even foul throw-ins, though their little arms weren't really up to it. He made them line up while he demonstrated the correct way.

Even his five-year-old daughter, Elizabeth, who was supposed to blow every time he told her, didn't escape his wrath. "I've warned you, Lib. If you bugger around any more I'll take the whistle."

His wife Barbara was duly grateful when they all trailed back to the house for the birthday tea, all nicely quietened and exhausted. He watched them getting stuck into the goodies then went into his front room and opened a bottle of champagne.

"What do you mean, I'm now coming on' all middle-class? You can say I live in a middle-class house. You can say I've got a middle-class car. Say what you bloody like. It's only your opinion. This house isn't middle-class. It's bloody Buckingham Palace.

"I'm still a Socialist and always will be, but that doesn't stop

me having the best car. I can get out three kids in it, plus the wife
and me Mam and Dad, all in comfort, that's why I have it. The
club car when I came here was a Vauxhall Victor, but I didn't
want that. I asked them to buy me a Mercedes last year but they
wouldn't. So I said stuff it, I'll buy one myself."

He says his Socialism is from the heart, not his head, and always
has been. Over the years he's been asked several times to stand as a
Labout M.P. and has seriously considered it. He has a charity box
for leukaemia research on the bar in his office. He's talked all his
staff into giving up part of their salaries to Oxfam. During the
miners' strike he gave out free tickets for Derby matches to the
pickets.

"I just have to read the papers to know I'm a Socialist. Look at
all the millions not being fed. Look at the political prisoners. Look
at the discrimination everywhere, not just colour but class, education and privilege of all sorts. I'm lucky. I've got three well fed,
superbly looked after kids. When I saw the pictures of those dead
kids in Biafra I burst into tears.

People in football are surprised I'm a Socialist. Their apathy
generally is staggering, which I think is an indictment of my
profession. They say sport and politics don't mix, which is rubbish.
It's like saying you don't need oxygen to breathe. You can't have
one without the other on this earth. I think people who want to
keep politics out of sport are a bit simple."

In practice as a manager he tries to follow his principles, such as
never discriminating, except against the louts and skivers. There's
one London team which has him frothing at the mouth, just
because he maintains a spiv element has been allowed to take over.
"If you threaten certain spiv players, you must carry it out and not
let them get away with it. A football team has only 11 players. It
just needs one bad 'un to affect the rest. In ICI, with thousands
and thousands of people, you can afford to carry some scoundrels.
Not in a football team."

He's fanatical about education, insisting that each apprentice
who joins the club at 15 goes to the local Polytechnic for one full
day and two evenings each week till he's a full professional. Most
managers allow young players time off for study, but not many
make it compulsory. "I can't guarantee to turn boys into professional footballers at Derby, but they'll end up well educated. I've
got one boy, 16-year-old Steve Powell, who's doing three A-levels.
I've got another doing a degree. In this democracy in which we
live, education is available to all despite the public schools trying
to make it exclusive. Give me any time a talented football player

who's also intelligent. Show me a talented player who's thick, and I'll show you a player with problems."

If his heart is therefore in the right place, if he's kind to children, contributes generously to charity and always helps dumb footballers across the road, why then do so many people dislike him?

It's all to do with his TV appearances. It's a bit ambivalent about why he goes on. One minute he says he loves it, admitting he laps it up and yes, he must be vain, and the next he's trying to pretend he does it as a duty, because it's an honour for Derby. "There are 92 football managers, give or take the six or seven who are about to be sacked every season, so I think it's a compliment to Derby that the BBC should choose me for their football panels."

There's no doubt he loves it, despite all the abuse he's had to take over the years. "I've had some terrible stick. I know many viewers say bloody hell, not that bugger again. But there's now been a complete switch. I'm not bulling you, because I never bull, but I promise you the letters have suddenly changed. They now say I'm right.

"The thing is, people never *listen* to what you say on the telly. All they notice is your manner. I can't help my voice. I can't help how I look. If people disagreed with what I say, that would be one thing, but it's *how* I say it that gets them."

Internally, his manner has led to a few rows in the BBC. He's not very good, for example, at controlling his bad language. He called Sir Alf Ramsey "a stubborn bugger". During the World Cup they put him with a panel of nine, which he thought was ridiculous. "It was a silly set-up so I just messed around. They then saw sense and agreed with me.

"I'm against any rehearsing and always refuse to do it. I've also refused to have Bob Wilson talking about managerial problems, not when I'm on anyway. He's a player and he knows nothing about management. I won't have it."

Now and again, when he sees himself as others see him, he's a bit appalled. "I came home once and watched a recording of a sports programme I'd been on. I thought, bloody hell, that's not me, is it. What a big-headed, dogmatic bastard. So next time I tried to calm down. It meant they got themselves a crappy interview.

"I only get upset if the wife's upset. She did once say I'd been extremely rude to someone. Sometimes I do set out to be rude, but that time I hadn't meant it. I hate me Mam getting upset, that's even worse.

"I suppose I've got more intelligent and wiser over the years, but I'm not going to try and change myself now. It doesn't bother me what people think.

"They say I've got chips on my shoulder, but I don't think so. I just believe in giving my opinion. I just say it's mine. They tell me that in giving my opinions I shout, but bloody hell, you've got to shout, when kids in Vietnam are having bombs dropped on them. O.K., I *have* got a chip on my shoulder, if it means shouting out about what's wrong with the world. And O.K., I'm stupid and ignorant enough to think my opinions *are* right. Have some more champagne. To absent friends, those buggers in London. You wouldn't believe the pleasure I've had out of drinking their health."

At 36, he's the youngest manager to win the First Division. Apart from walking on the water, or being Prime Minister, what else is there to do?

"I wouldn't mind being Prime Minister. I wouldn't take the yacht, but I'd have a go at it, if I thought I could do it. So far all I've found I can do is be a football manager. I can't see myself doing this for ever. I can't visualise myself at the age of 55 still in this game. At times I do think I'll give it up. Times like when we get beat at home. Times when I've got to go out and spend £200,000 on a player. Times when I have to go into the dressing room and shout at them, knowing that one of these days some player is going to say balls to you, and walk out on me.

"I have thought about getting out of football altogether, now that I've won something. But I've only been a manager seven years. I'm only on the threshold of my career. I've got a lifetime to go. I got cheated as a player. I don't want to be cheated as a manager."

From *The Sunday Times Magazine*, 1973

151

The Thing
He Loves

Brian Glanville

How did it *feel*, John?

It felt terrible. The worst moment in my life, it felt. It still does.

It always will. It's going to be with me forever, this; the moment.
Sleeping and waking. Dreaming about it. Then waking up,
remembering about it. Through the windscreen, out of the pelting
rain, suddenly this figure rushing. And thinking these two things,
me: or rather one thing, and under it another.

. First, bloody hell, he's mad, what's he doing? And under it,
right in the same split second, a sort of, somehow, *recognising*.
But all of it happening so quick; bang on the footbrake, then that
dreadful bump. Oh, Christ, I've hit him. Getting out of the car,
all shaking, then seeing him there, his body, and the shock again,
this time the double shock, the body and the blood. Slumped over,
with his back to me. And then the other feeling, stronger, suddenly,
recognising. God, please God, don't let it, don't let it be him, it
can't be him. And sort of hearing people's voices: "Joe . . . It's
Joey Black . . . Joe's dead . . . He's killed Joey." Then click: passing
out.

Coming round, there was this big policeman, holding me. Rain
in my face. "What happened, son?" And the voices again: "It's
Joey Black . . . Dead . . . Joey . . . Saw it all; he run out like a
lunatic . . . Ay, but he could've stopped."

I said, "Is that right? Have I killed Joey Black?" And him, "All
right, keep back, you lot. Now, what exactly happened, son?"

I asked him, "Is he *dead*? You've got to tell me, is he dead?"
I think I went a bit hysterical, struggling away from him, standing
up, trying to get over and see the body, but he stopped me, he
hauled me back, I could just see all that mass of long fair hair, the
blood around, then an ambulance came jangling up, folk scattering.
They jumped out, threw a blanket over, and lifted him on a stretcher,
then aboard, away, jangling. He was gone. Nothing in the road
now but this patch of blood, washing away fast in the rain, dis-
appearing in the gutter.

I said, "It *was* Joe, wasn't it, and he's dead." He said, "Ay, son, I'm afraid so," and it swept over me again, this faintness, but I shook it off, I fought it. In fact this was it; the worst moment in my life, because it was empty now, my life was, completely empty, nothing left of it, like they'd scooped me out inside and left the shell of me. I said, "It *can't* be," though I knew by now it was, it just *seemed* so impossible, seeing him play that very afternoon, just a few hours before. *Him*; and me, that worshipped him, that lived to see him play, that would have given myself in his place, any day.

They took me home in a police car. I walked through the door, a copper on either side of me; my mother's face, she couldn't understand it; I'd never been in trouble in my life.

I said, "I've killed him; Joey Black," not thinking what I said, and she tottered, then one of the coppers said, "A motor accident it was; Market Square," and they put me to bed. I lay there, not ever wanting to get up again.

Has it changed your life in any way, John?
It *has* changed my life. It's changed it in a lot of ways.

One way it changed it, right from the first, was that it wasn't worth living, now. How could I face things? How was I going to face people?

Waking that first morning. Something black weighing on me, crushing me down. Remembering it, then. Snapping on the light above my bed, and seeing *him* looking straight at me from across the room, the lifesize photo of him in the City colours. And wherever I turned, to whichever wall, everywhere, there he was, staring at me, head and shoulders, action shots, or from out of a team group. Sometimes with long hair, sometimes with it shorter, from his early days, when he just got in the team. It was worse than anywhere, my room was, the accident came back and back to me, the rain, him running, then the thump, his body, till I hurried out into the bathroom, and I locked myself in there.

It was still early, only six o'clock. I stayed in there an hour or so, trying not to think about the accident, but if it wasn't the accident it was still him, Joey, running like he always used to run, shirt outside his shorts, the long hair flapping, dodging and swerving in the way he had, swaying over the ball, or sometimes scoring. The last goal he got – *that* came back to me – the one on Saturday, because it was the last; he'd never get another. I'd done for him.

I sat there: I was paralysed. I couldn't go out anywhere, I couldn't stay in. If I went out, they'd all be staring at me, it was bound to be in the papers by now. There he is, that's him, the one that killed Joe Black. And whatever I told them – I'm a City fan, I idolised him, I admired him as much as you ever did – none of that would make tuppence worth of difference, none of it could alter what I'd done, even if I never meant it.

But if I stayed home, in my room, there it all was, the dozens of reminders. I went back in there, thinking that I'd take them down, and the first thing I went to was the lifesize photo. I started unpinning it, to put it somewhere, then I stopped; I couldn't go on. His face was smiling at me, and I found I was seeing two things at once, not just the cardboard photo but his actual body, sprawled like it had been in the road.

I sat down on the bed and didn't move; I don't know how long I'd been there when my mother came in. She was in her dressing-gown, she'd brought a cup of tea, she said, "You couldn't help it, John," and then I started crying, it seemed to touch something off. I said, "I know I couldn't, I know I couldn't," tears all running down my face. I couldn't take the tea from her. I said, "Suddenly bang: like that. From nowhere. Right in front of me."

She said, "I know, I know, the policeman said it wasn't *your* fault."

I said, "But it *was* my fault. I was driving, wasn't I? It was my car, wasn't it? It was me hit him, didn't I?"

She said, "If it hadn't been you, it would have been the next car."

I said, "What next car? Why should it? He'd have got across, he'd have been safe, he'd be alive to play."

Which set me off thinking about my car; a 1960 Morris Oxford it was that I'd picked up for a hundred quid and been so proud of; that I'd worked and worked on, God knows how many hours, stripping down the engine, fitting new parts until I think the whole damn thing must have been new, and all for this, this one moment in the Market Square.

When the old man came in later on and told me that the police had phoned, I could pick up the car on Monday from where it was in the pound, I said, "Leave it there. I never want to see it again."

He said, "Your *car?*" like he couldn't believe it. I said, "It's not my bloody car," and I thought of it sitting there in the police pound with, and this was the worst thing, the blue City sticker on its back window and the little blue City doll that hung in the windscreen, then of the dent there'd be in the front wing, maybe the bumper, and what that meant. I knew I could never drive that

*"You're a fanatic, Willy. Stranded, and all you want to do is follow
a crowd to another match."*

car again. I didn't think that I'd ever *drive* again, come to that.

He stood there, the old man, looking at me, not talking, till in
the end he asked me, "Are you going to work tomorrow?" I
said, "No." He said, "You can't sit here the rest of your life." I
said, "Leave me alone." He said, "Your breakfast's waiting on the
table." I said, "Just leave me alone."

Wasn't Joey Black your favourite player, John?
He was everybody's favourite player, wasn't he?

Every City fan's; and lots that weren't City fans. There'll never
be another like him. The goals he scored, the way he could go
past people. A goal he got against Arsenal; he must have gone
round four defenders, all of them trying to chop him down, him
swaying and swerving; inside one, outside the next, then when it
looked like he was right off balance, shooting with the near foot as
he fell, instead of bringing through the back foot, right across the
goalkeeper and low into the opposite corner. I can run that through
my mind like a film, every step of it. I'd never seen a goal to touch
it, and I knew I never would again unless *he* scored it; jammed in at
the Kop end with all the others, all of us shouting the "Joey-Joey-
Joey!" chant, then falling down the terraces like an avalanche,

155

which could have been frightening. But it wasn't, it was marvellous; people were laughing, not screaming. Right out of control we were, it was like being carried by a great big wave, you didn't know when the hell you'd stop and yet you didn't care, you were only sorry when you did stop.

Five days I stayed in my room. I didn't shave, I hardly ate. Reporters came; television, and all, but I wouldn't see them. I told my mother, send them away, they're like vultures.

Ted came round, my married brother. He said, "You weren't to blame, John, everyone's agreed on it. He ran out, there was no way you could stop yourself in time. As if *you'd* purposely have done a thing like that. You'd be the very last."

I said, "Everyone?" I said, "How the hell do *they* know? If I'd not been there, it would never have happened. And that's all that counts."

The one person I thought about at all, other than *him*, was Louise. Not at first. I was too numb at first with all the shock of it. Just dead to everything. Then when I did start thinking about her I thought, she's sure to finish with me, now, with how she'd felt about Joey: it'll be the end of *that*, as well. And I accepted it; how else could it be when he'd been so big in both our lives, Joey, when she went on him as much as I did, more in a way, with her being a girl, and girls all liking him so much. She'd as many pictures of him stuck up on her wall at home as I had, including the lifesize, and others of him on the beach, on holiday in Italy.

She'd been with me on Saturday, on the terraces; she'd been with me that day against the Arsenal, too, we'd been swept right down together, holding on to one another, laughing.

Then she did come. My mother said, "It's Louise; will you see her?" And first I had this sort of shock – *she's here, Louise!* – bringing me back to life, then I went numb again, then in the end I said, "Okay, I'll see her."

She came in and at first she just stood there. She was wearing her blue and white City scarf, like she always did. She said. "I'd have been before. Your mother said you didn't want to see anyone."

I was sitting in a chair, I didn't get up, I was looking down at the floor. She said, "It wasn't *your* fault, John."

"I know," I said, "they've told me that."

She said, "As if *you'd* do a thing like that; of all people, you." and I said, "I'd have cut my leg off, I'd have changed places with him, honest."

She said, "I know you would, John," and she took my hand, which set me off crying, again. Yet at the same time I was wondering

156

how could I ever marry her now when she'd always bring it back to me, more than anybody else.

The doctor came once or twice. He gave me pills to take, tranquilisers, and a letter to the bank so I wouldn't have to go back. Then there was another copper came; he wasn't bad, he stood there in the middle of the room in his big policeman's boots, asking me questions about the accident, taking things down in his book. He told me there was going to be an inquest, and when I heard that I could have died, I really wanted to die. Having to go through it all again, the whole thing again, and in public, with people looking at me. What were they going to say, what would they do to me, because he was God here, was Joey.

Did you find people blamed you?

Some did, yes, some blamed me; but no worse than I blamed myself. They couldn't do.

In court there was his father and mother; that was the worst of it. They'd come down from Scotland and they sat there in the court-room, looking at me, you did it, you killed him, it was you run over Joey. Every time I met their eyes, it was like being stabbed. I wanted to explain, I wanted to come down from that witness-box and tell them, that I'd *loved* Joey, that I'd worshipped Joey, that I'd do anything, literally, to make him come alive again . . . that I wished it had been me instead of him. Only I could tell that they just wouldn't listen. Even when the verdict was given, death by misadventure, they kept on looking at me just the same; I couldn't blame them. After all, I'd killed him, hadn't I? Whatever the coroner said, whether I'd done it on purpose or I hadn't.

I wrote to them after, trying to explain things, but I never got any answer. They'd even had this lawyer to question me. What speed was I doing when exactly had I seen him and why was I so slow in putting on the brakes? Ridiculous questions that couldn't possibly do any good; trying to catch me, playing games with me. What's the point of it? I kept on thinking, what's the use? As if all this can bring him back again. If they could only do that, they could jail me for life, I'd go willingly. They could even hang me if they wanted.

And *my* parents, on the other side of the court from what they were, looking at them now and then, but them never looking back. They tried to talk to them once, outside the court, but apparently those two, they just turned their back and walked off. "As if you were a criminal," my mother said, "as if you'd for a minute meant it."

157

The plans I made then, when it was all going on. To emigrate; to start a new life in Australia, or maybe Canada. To join the Merchant Navy. To change my name, and go to London. I wouldn't go back to the bank, not until after the inquest, and even then I wasn't sure if I would.

That first morning, when I did go back, I remember coming in, not looking left or right, feeling them watching me, all of them; everything dead silent. I went through behind the counter, hung up my coat in the cloak-room there, went over and stood at my old window, and Ron Baker, that was beside me, said, "Are you all right then, John?" and I said, "Ay, I'm all right."

The whole of that day they never once mentioned what had happened, any of them. It would have been better in a way if they had, because saying nothing made it worse, it hung there in the air, glances, whispering. There were the customers, too, I'd been dreading them the most of all, having to face them, one after the other; when I counted the notes, my hands were shaking. A few of them said: "Glad to see you back," but most of them just looked at me like I was a freak, something you paid to see in a circus, a bit frightened, as if they were afraid I might harm them.

I walked out at lunch and I went home. I told my mother that I'd never go back, I couldn't face it, but they were quite good about it; they found me a clerical job away from the counter and I stayed in the end, but it was terrible, still. I felt as though I'd lost a skin. Those days, I don't know how I got through them. It was like the bottom had dropped out of my life, the centre of it.

Before, well, everything really had been the City. The morning papers and the evening papers. Who they were going to play that week, who was in and who was dropped, who was fit and who was hurt, who they were trying to buy and who they'd sell, the Football Green on a Saturday night, the match reports on the Sunday morning, Match of the Day on telly on the Saturday night, especially if it was City on. The away games, travelling all over the country, up to Newcastle and down to London, or even abroad, flying, if they were playing in Europe. We'd been as far as Naples once, Louise and me.

Now I couldn't bear to hear their name even mentioned, the City, and as for *his* name, it was like a knife in me. But wherever I went I'd think I'd hear it; in the street, on buses, in the cafes. Or see it, catching sight of people's newspapers, even though nine times out of 10 I'd be wrong. I'd look closer and see it was some other name.

Then there was the Supporters Club. Before, we'd meet every

week, our branch, every Friday night; I was the assistant secretary. I sent them a letter round saying I resigned, and three of them came round and called, two of them and Louise. They told me the same old thing, it wasn't my fault, they knew it was an accident, they said, "We know you're just as upset by it as what we are." But I told them no, I'd never come back, I wanted to put it all behind me, forget there was ever such a thing as City. They looked at me like they couldn't believe it. Another thing was I admit I was scared, I was afraid I'd be attacked. In the street, I was forever hearing footsteps behind, especially if I was out. I thought that if I ever went near the stadium they'd get me for certain. But I still felt like I was paralysed, which was why I didn't leave, didn't change my job, didn't emigrate, didn't go to London, didn't do any of the things I'd thought about. The centre wasn't there any more, and because it wasn't there, I couldn't act, I just couldn't move.

One night, when Louise came round and my mother and father were both out I went to bed with her and I couldn't do anything, the first time it had ever happened to me. In the end, I lost control of myself, I started shouting at her, "Get out, go home, I don't ever want to see you again!" I don't know what happened to me.

Except that she was so much a part of it.

Mr Gray, I believe it's a year since you were involved in that tragic accident.

A year since the death of Joey Black, yes.

And today, before the kick-off at the City ground, you placed a wreath on the centre spot in his memory.

That's correct, yes.

How did it feel?

It was the proudest moment of my life.

The proudest I've ever known, the proudest I ever *will* know. Sixty thousand of them, all of them cheering me as I walked out there with the flowers, cheering me, and through me, cheering *him*. What they were saying was that they'd forgiven me. It was so different from the first time I'd gone back after it had happened.

After three months. Only through Louise telling and telling me: "You've got to go, you must go," and me turning her down, because every time I even thought about it it would make me feel sick, even the idea of the place. The floodlight pylons, which were always the first thing that you'd see when you drove up the Lancaster Road, thrusting up over the roofs, then the rosette sellers and the newspaper placards and inside, inside the ground itself, the pitch; maybe green at the beginning of the season, rich and smooth, then thick and muddy, in the winter, then, by the spring, all patchy, brown, most of it, just fringed with green along the touchlines. And him not there; them coming out of the tunnel without him, the cheer sounding different, I *knew* it would sound different. The disappointment, the crowd half-hoping he'd be there again, a miracle would happen and he'd trot out with them, that long hair bobbing up and down, knees coming up high, the way they did when he ran on to the field. Nine, 10, 11 and not one of them him, with me there knowing it was my fault that he wasn't.

I wore a balaclava helmet that day, the only time I've ever worn one in my life; a balaclava helmet and on top of that a trilby hat with the brim pulled down, like a gangster. We didn't stand the Kop end, either, like we always used to, in among all the regulars, I couldn't bring myself to face them yet; we stood the other end, behind the Crawford Road goal. I was frightened to death I'd be recognised, that they'd go for me, because there'd been all these phone calls and letters, some of the things they said you'd not believe, the filth that can pout out of people. Three in the morning the phone rang once; I went downstairs and there was this voice, "John Gray?" I said, "Yes, what is it?" and it said, "We'll kill you, you bastard, we're coming round to get you," and others, too, and all those terrible letters. I thought to myself then, if they only knew; because what could they do worse to me than what I was doing to myself? The end of it was we had to change our phone number.

They did bad at first, City, after Joey died, lost the next three on the trot. I tried not to find out what was happening but you couldn't avoid it. The thing seemed to weigh on the whole city, it was like a fog, everyone seemed to be living in mourning. You could tell it from the way they walked, their faces, the tone of their voice. People seemed to talk low, they mumbled, and I know I wasn't just imagining it, it wasn't only me. In fact when you're as low as what I was, you notice things a lot more, you're sensitive to things.

I didn't go to his funeral because they had it in Scotland, but I went to the memorial service they had here a few weeks after; on my own, right at the back. There was hundreds there in the Cathedral, a lot of them crying, and when it came to the part about men growing up and being cut down I went cold, I couldn't move, it felt like everybody in the whole Cathedral had turned round and was looking at me; *you* did it, *you* did it, look at him, there he is.

But it passed, and then we sang *Abide With Me*, like at the Cup Final, and suddenly for the first time I begun to feel better, I honestly believe that was the turning point. Hundreds of us, all singing, all City fans, like we might have sung *You'll Never Walk Alone* on the terraces. We were together in what we felt, in what Joey had been to us.

And the sermon was beautiful too; it was preached by the Dean, a tall old fellow with a big, hooked nose and a ring of white hair, he talked about them that the gods loved dying young, he said that Joey's life had been perfect in a way, this was how we ought to think of it, because he'd gone out on the crest, we'd always remember him as a shining star of the football field, somebody who'd lived and died a hero.

I came out of that church and I can't tell you how I felt, different than I'd felt for weeks, like something, some great burden, had been lifted, I was alive again. There were other things he said that kept coming back to me, how we were all part of a great scheme, every one of us, how none of us could understand it but each one of us had our part in it, and I thought about this a lot, I realised I was in it, too, and gradually it came to me that maybe this was meant to happen, maybe there was a purpose to even this; and day by day, things changed.

I thought about it all, about him, just as much as I ever had, but now it was in a different sort of way, the way the old Dean had talked about, not so much mourning for him now as *remembering* him, thinking of him as he *had* been, at his best, scoring goals, flying past tackles, all the things he'd meant and done, when he was still playing.

I rang Louise and met her again, in a cafe because I didn't want to be alone with her yet, but it went quite well, in fact a lot better. She was pleased to see me, I was happy to be with her. A week or so later she did come round and this time everything was right.

One day I put his picture up again; the lifesize one. I'd not destroyed it; it was in a cupboard under the stairs with all the rest of the stuff, the photos and the rosettes and the banners, the blanket that had all the club badges on, 200 of them, the 5,000 programmes. I couldn't bring myself to chuck them all away, especially the photographs of *him*, it would have been like sacrilege, but I couldn't bring myself to look at them, either, so that's where they were, that's where they'd stayed. I waited for Louise to come before I put it up again, the lifesize, I wanted it to be a kind of little ceremony, and she realised this. We put it up together, then we sat on the bed holding hands, looking at it for a while, then we made love.

John, it was you who initiated the Joe Black Memorial Award?
  It was, yes.
  Was this your way of making amends?
  I suppose you could say that.
  And what does the award consist of?
  It consists of the sum of £50 and a silver statuette of Joe Black, in action, which is presented every year to the young City player who, in the opinion of the Joe Black Memorial Award Committee of the Supporters Club, has shown most promise during that season.

That first match. The feeling when they came out, and no Joey with them, the emptiness. I knew Louise could tell how I felt, because she gripped my hand, but when the game began, the feeling went away.

I watched at first without a sound, which wasn't like me at all. In the old days I'd have joined in all the chants, I'd be yelling my head off. But suddenly they scored, right down our end, woosh! A lovely shot, the ball bulging the top of the net out right in front of us, and that released it. I shouted, it was like a spell that had been broken. From that moment, I was shouting to the very end.

We won 3–1, it was Everton we beat, and I think this showed me something else, that there'd *always* be a City, any road for as long as *we* could see, just as there *had* been one for nearly 90 years; long before Joey, long before me, long before even my old man had stood on these same terraces. City went on and life went on and *I* went on, and as for Joey Black, I realised that the important thing now was that people mustn't forget him. That was my duty, now, to see they didn't, to preserve his memory; that was how I could make up for what I'd done.

The very next Supporters Club meeting, I went down there, and told them what I'd thought. They were all of them very nice to me, they asked me: "Why haven't you been before, lad?" They thought it was a wonderful idea and when we announced it there was a lot of publicity, articles in the papers and all. The money came pouring in and we had this beautiful statuette made, Joey running with the ball at his feet, just like him, just about to kick it, taken from a photograph.

The first season I presented it myself to the kid who'd took Joey's place, Colin Brooks; they had the telly cameras there and I don't know how many reporters. I'd been afraid before that I'd not be able to speak, but when the time come I did, it just came pouring out, a tribute to Joey, what he'd been to all of us, how no one had admired him more than me but what we were here for now was to honour his memory and use it as an inspiration to help City and the players that came after him, because that was what Joey himself would want.

Do you still think about the accident at all, John?

Now and again, yes. But you can't go back in life or football, can you? You must go forward.

From *The Thing He Loves and other stories*, 1973

Allez Hampton

Alan Simpson

Being programme notes from Hampton Football Club Programme as penned by its president:

As another season draws to a close it is traditional to look back over the past few months, but I think this year it is more relevant to look forward.

There is no doubt that the game is going to change dramatically in the next few years, and the biggest change is going to come now that Grocer Heath has managed to drag us into the Common Market.

What's that got to do with football you may ask. You're joking! The whole game as we know it is going to be affected. The fact that we invented it isn't going to make the slightest bit of difference. To explain how these changes are going to come about we must have a look at the Treaty of Rome.

First of all, free exchange of labour. That's half our team gone for a start. Jeff Sillett will be playing for Benidorm Park Rangers. And I know for a fact that Andy Welsted and Simon Johnson have already had offers from Duisberg North End. And on terms that we at Hampton cannot possibly match. Three pfennigs a mile petrol money, two marks 50 meal money on training nights, and free admission to the Golden Anchor. Mind you, two nights in the Golden Anchor and I wouldn't fancy their chances of reaching the touchline.

Nevertheless, we at Hampton have to protect ourselves against these wogs from across the Channel nicking all our brightest talent by inveighling them to the fleshpots of Europe. Rest assured your committee have not remained idle in this matter. Classes have already started in the club-house, conducted by Madammoiselle Fifi de la Crumpet, Folies Bergere (1929), in which the entire Ladies Committee are being instructed in the art of serving a tray-load of pints of draught Guinness in the bar, topless, without making any indents in the creamy bit on top. Ribald remarks from their husbands such as, "She'd have a job knocking over a sherry glass," are being discouraged.

Your secretary is doing his best. Although personally I feel that a Basque beret, Alpine shorts and clogs do not give the best impression when one is defending a player in front of the Middlesex F.A. Disciplinary Committee at the Ealing Town Hall.

Our Manager, Herr von Philpott, as he is now known, thinks he is helping by training the players to employ the goosestep at all times during the game. All this has succeeded in doing so far is to ensure that eight players have been sent off for going over the top of the ball. But as Herr von Philpott rightly screams on training nights: "Today the Isthmian League, tomorrow the WORLD!"

Your treasurer, Monsieur Alain le Duddy, has probably been the most successful in perfecting the changeover. Where else in the world, other than Hampton Football Club, can foreign visitors get such incredible rates of exchange as 3·50 Deutschmarks to the pound, plus duty free Scotch to take back home at five and a half quid a bottle? Bien fait, Monsieur le Duddy, F.C. Hampton, est dead chuffed avec vous.

The Italian aspect of the changeover has not been overlooked. Every Tuesday night throughout the close season, our coach will be taking the entire playing staff in singing lessons on the training pitch. We look forward to next season when a reprimanded player faced with an irate referee will be supported by the entire team surrounding the official singing "*Cara Mia Mine*".

Naturally, all our efforts to Europeanise the club will be of no avail without the help of our supporters. May I offer a few guiding lines to what you should do in the future?

First of all, the chants. "*Go home, you bums,*" should in future be replaced by "*Allez vous-en, vous derrieres*"; "*We want a riot*" should now become "*Nous voulons un punch-up*"; "*The referee is a . . . . !*" is now changed to "*L'arbitre est un . . . . !*". It's quite easy when you get used to it. Finally, a glossary of terms which might come in handy when the game becomes Common Marketised:

Hand ball! – Malle de Main! (Or wittily reduced to "Balmain", the famous dress designer, thus implying that the visitors are a bunch of poufs.)

Man up your back! – Homme sur votre queue! (If this happens the game should be abandoned and the culprits reported immediately to the local watch committee. There is a limit to what we English can tolerate from these barbarians.)

Coup de grace – Get the bleeding grass cut. (This is for groundsmen only.)

Free kick – Coup a libre! (Or, rendered down, Cuba Libri. So the next time you see our players in the bar getting stoned on rum and coke, you know they are merely discussing the merits of the free kick that was awarded against them in the last minute, and the barman has completely misunderstood them.)

However, tonight we welcome the players, officials and supporters of Hendon F.C. (F.C. Poule de Professeur) in the first leg (Premier Jambe) of the Middlesex Senior Cup (Coupe d'ancien ginger beers). And may the best team win. There's no equivalent to that on the other side of the Channel.

From the *Hampton Football Club programme*

Leeds v. Sunderland, 1973

Geoffrey Green

In spite of all the myriad words written and spoken in advance, Wembley on Saturday in the end provided an emotional FA Cup Final of live theatre with no script. It was played from the heart and it was Sunderland, with a goal by Porterfield just after the half-hour, whose heart finally proved the bigger as they knocked down the giant of Leeds United, the holders and odds-on favourites.

Not since 1928 when Blackburn Rovers, struggling against relegation, beat Huddersfield Town, their own eyes on the double, has there been such a jumbo-sized upset in a final. Some of course might prefer to point to Portsmouth's defeat of the heavily fancied Wolverhampton Wanderers in 1939. But that is a mere academic point.

The real point was that here we had a triumph for the game itself, for the underdog, and for the unashamed romantics all on a grey, wet afternoon when Wembley's 50th birthday was celebrated in champagne fashion. So Sunderland became the first Second Division side to lift the prize in 42 years and the voice of the north-east was raised over the nation's capital. As well it might, for not once in seven visits to the stadium by Newcastle and Sunderland has the north-east been left empty-handed.

Once again, logic was put to flight, and Leeds cannot complain. They had their chances for victory but on the day – jaded, perhaps, after all their strenuous efforts in the League and in Europe – they were not big enough to grasp them. Even Bremner and Giles, frustrated and short of ideas the longer the battle went, fell into the mistake of lobbing high passes into the Sunderland penalty area where they were firmly dispatched by the tall head of Watson, an impossible giant of a centre-half and on my card the man of the match with Madeley.

Any post mortem, however, might question that judgement and point instead to Montgomery the Sunderland goalkeeper. Certainly it was he who provided the final turning point with an unbelievable save from Lorimer quite the equal of Banks's famous effort against Pele in the World Cup.

In fact, there were two saves in one as it were and it all happened at the psychological moment midway through the second half. At that point, Leeds, with 10 men on the hunt, were turning the screw tighter and tighter as Sunderland's resistance at last seemed to be draining away. Giles began the move: Reaney took up the pattern, crossed deep from the right and there was Cherry catapulting in from the left to plant a fierce header to the far corner. Somehow Montgomery palmed it out but straight into the path of the oncoming Lorimer. All the Leeds man needed to do was push the ball calmly home for the equaliser. Instead he blasted it from six yards range but somehow Montgomery, still flat on the ground, put up an arm in reflex action like a man trying to ward off a blow, to divert the shot on to the crossbar and away. In that moment Leeds died. It was the final act and Sunderland were home, almost scoring again in the last seconds when Harvey pushed away a shot by Halom after Tueart and Kerr had ripped open the stretched Leeds defence.

Yorkshire, too, might feel aggrieved about one other moment some 10 minutes after the interval when Watson hooked up Bremner inside the area. It looked all over a penalty but perhaps Bremner's own past told against him instinctively as the referee dismissed the swift passage with an imperious wave of the arm.

Certainly it would have been cruel had all Sunderland's spirited, talented offering been brought to nothing from the penalty spot. Much of their football was gay and full of unexpected angles which had even Hunter and Madeley going the wrong way at times.

Hughes and Tueart were the mobile, sharp prongs up front: Kerr, inexhaustible and leader by example, ran himself into the ground as he hunted midfield and dropped back also to help eliminate Gray, the expected danger man, later substituted by Yorath. Horswill nagged Giles like a terrier from first to last: Bremner was similarly harried and hurried by Porterfield to break the Leeds rhythm.

It was an all round team effort, skilful, spirited and free from fear. With nothing to lose, Sunderland, keeping the ball on the ground handsomely, actually seemed to enjoy themselves in the way football should be enjoyed. But at the heart of it all was Watson, the pillar of authority, and behind him Montgomery, a goalkeeper of instinct. Each earned an extra medal.

It was Watson's tall challenge in the air, assisted by Halom, to Hughes's corner from the left that actually opened up the goal. As the ball came down to Porterfield, he killed the bounce with his

168

left thigh and swivelled elegantly to crash in his shot with his right.

Harvey's net puffed, the west bank of the stadium exploded into a canvas of red and stayed that way until the end. The voice of the north-east provided a wall of noise and there at the finish was Bob Stokoe, the Sunderland manager, first joyfully embracing his goalkeeper and then finding himself chaired by his team as the Cup headed for Wearside again after a lapse of 36 years.

It was Sunderland's hour after hour after hour. As for Leeds, tired, but unbowed, they move on to another final in the European Cup Winners' Cup feeling perhaps that nine times out of 10 they could have kept their trophy won last spring. But this was the 10th time and it is good for the game that these things should happen.

SUNDERLAND: J. Montgomery; D. Malone, R. Guthrie, M. Horswill, D. Watson, R. Pitt, R. Kerr, W. Hughes, V. Halom, I. Porterfield, D. Tueart.

LEEDS UNITED: D. Harvey; P. Reaney, T. Cherry, W. Bremner, P. Madeley, N. Hunter, P. Lorimer, A. Clarke, M. Jones, J. Giles, E. Gray (sub: T. Yorath).

From *The Times*, 1973

Scapegoats

Leslie Vernon

Relax boys, everything is O.K. with football! The UEFA Committee who have been trying to find ways and means of breaking the defensive deadlock, can now be disbanded. The chairmen's meeting in London was an unnecessary waste of time and money, the world-wide investigations for a solution may be discontinued.

Gordon Lee, manager of the much-admired Port Vale F.C. has found the answer and has put the finger on the guilty men – the football writers. Mr Lee says that it is bad publicity which created "the alarming gulf that exists between clubs and the paying public".

He writes in the League Review: "The game's good points are hidden and completely overruled by bad publicity. Frankly, I am not interested in the number of bookings and sending-offs, arrests and trouble spots. If I had a belated New Year's wish, it would be to stifle the pens of those who can write nothing but wrong about football. I hope they stop and think next time they pick up their poisoned pens."

It had to happen, of course. After all, the usual excuses had been exhausted, a new scapegoat had to be found. Mr Lee is perfectly right. I myself witnessed Geoffrey Green of The Times viciously tackling an opponent from behind, Desmond Hackett swearing at the referee, and Brian James handling his ball-point pen deliberately.

It is the journalists who wreck trains, stab visiting supporters, throw toilet paper rolls on the pitch, refuse to sit 10 yards from a free-kick, and commit diabolical tactical fouls. Most of them are trained ventriloquists who use the managers as their dummies, and through them give instructions to the players which are contrary to the spirit of the game.

Port Vale has impeccable credentials. They played against West Ham in a recent cup tie so scandalously that the usually placid Ron Greenwood had to wait three days to calm down and tell the full story to the reporter of "The Hammers" local paper. "I wanted our supporters to know what happened. We were intimidated outrageously – even Bobby Moore was frightened. They were trying to kick us off the park."

Well, dear Mr Lee, how is that for creating gulfs and giving football a bad name! Should we have suppressed this information or have written the truth first as Greenwood saw it, then as you did? You might not be interested in the arrests, trouble spots, or the number of bookings. But the police are, and the clubs must be, because they are losing players through suspensions. I for one will give my poisoned pen a rest, and supply fellow scribes with a new-style match report to copy.

RESULTS: Muggers Utd. o   Mafia F.C. o
REFEREE: B. F. Falstaff (deceased after 72 mins, play).
ATTENDANCE: 371

"On my way to the ground, I noticed that the visiting supporters were greeted with expressions of love and kindness by the home fans. Small gifts, mementoes, and girl friends, were also exchanged. The crowd was 34,000 fewer than last season, but as the fixture was played so soon after the Chinese New Year, and had clashed with the local flower show, this small drop was understandable.

"In brilliant sunshine, on a perfect pitch, the home team won the toss, and it was only due to a small misunderstand that the skipper threw the visiting captain in the air instead of the coin proffered to him by the good-looking tall (5 ft 4 in) referee, who good-humouredly wiped his bi-focals before the kick-off.

"The game itself was poetry in motion mainly slow motion. The play was confined to the centre-circle, but even in this confined space, these magnificent footballers did extraordinary things. Some with the ball, others without it. Unfortunately, the ref forgot to take the whistle out of his mouth, and every time he breathed out, he gave a free-kick (78 to the Muggers, 1 to Mafia).

"These constant interruptions provided the crowd with an opportunity to admire the nearby railway track, which was freshly painted in 1935. The Muggers' goalkeeper (father of two bouncing boys, a teetotaller and a churchgoer) wasn't busy, and had time to seal up some envelopes which contained goodwill messages to the Pope, Golda Meir and Norman Hunter.

"In the second half, the Mafia goal was under constant pressure, but they had plenty of protection. The referee awarded a controversial corner against the visitors in the 72nd minute, and the Mafia centre-back ran over to congratulate him. There was an accidental collision, and apparently the unfortunate official stabbed himself with his pencil. Senior linesman Al Lergic took over.

"This game demonstrated what is best in British football . . . 90 minutes non-stop effort, breathtaking centre-circle incidents, and a sporting spirit which is the envy of the world. After the match,

"Here he is and he doesn't look too happy!"

"Four–nil! No, FIVE–NIL?"

"Let's see now . . . they lost! . . . they were thrashed ! ! !"

"George, your face is a picture. Don't ever try and hide anything from me, love."

both managers told me that the opposition played better, and that they were lucky to get a point. The supporters mingled happily with the visiting fans, and arm-in-arm they sang a short chorus of Auld Lang Syne."

Does this suit you Mr Lee? Or shall we continue to write the truth . . .

From *World Soccer* '73

Skinner

Michael Parkinson

Cup-ties were different from other games. If Barnsley won we went to the pictures in the best seats, but if they lost there was sometimes a punch-up and the old man would come home from the boozer with a skinful saying the beer was off.

Barnsley, of course, used to be a good cup-fighting side. They only won the Cup once and that was in 1912, but they've never forgotten it and many a team from a higher division has been slain by them on that ground with the muck stacks peeping over the paddock. The reason for Barnsley's success in the Cup was, more often than not, that their game remained unchanged throughout years of tactical innovation. The team was both blind and deaf to subtleties like the bolt defence, the wall pass, 4–2–4 and deeply-lying centre forwards. Their game was founded rock solid on two basic principles best summed up by the exhortations of their supporters to "Get stuck in" or, alternatively, "Get rid".

During one spectacular cup run after the war, when Barnsley had beaten a First Division side, the old man held forth on the team's virtues on the bus going home. What he said was: "They'll take some stopping, yon team. They'll kick 'owt that moves." The bus agreed.

This love of hard combative graft above all else was not in any way unique among the supporters who Saturday after Saturday had their weekend-end mood dictated by how their team fared. Their unanimous favourites were the hard men who got stuck in and got rid without thought for the game's niceties. The odd sophisticates who crept into the team were tolerated but never loved. Thus they will tell you even now that Danny Blanchflower once played for Barnsley, but that he wasn't a patch on Skinner Normanton.

Normanton, I suppose, personified Barnsley's cup-fighting qualities. He was tough, tireless, aggressive, with a tackle as swift and spectacular as summer lighting. In the family tree of football his grandfather was Wilf Copping, his godson is Nobby Stiles. And just in case anyone is still uncertain about what kind of player he was, he could claim a distant link with Rocky Marciano. He was a miner and built like one. Billiard-table legs and a chest like the front of a coal barge. He was so fearsome that there are those who will tell you that naughty children in and around Barnsley were warned by their parents, "If you don't be good we'll send for Skinner."

The other legend about him, probably equally true, was that certain inside forwards of delicate constitution were known to develop nervous rashes and mysterious stomach disorders when faced with the prospect of a Saturday afternoon's sport with Skinner in opposition.

Cup-ties were his speciality, inside forwards with international reputations were his meat. He clinched one game for Barnsley in a manner all his very own. There was about 10 minutes to go, the scores level, and Barnsley were awarded a penalty. The inside forward placed the ball on the spot and as he turned to walk back Skinner, from the halfway line, set off running. The inside forward, ready to turn to take the kick, saw Skinner approaching like an odds-on favourite and wisely stepped aside. From that moment the grey, dour ground was lit with the purple and gold of pure fantasy. Without slackening speed Skinner kicked the ball with his toe-end. And, as he did, many things happened: the bar started shaking and humming, the goalkeeper fell to his face stunned and the ball appeared magically in the back of the net. What in fact had happened was that Skinner's shot had struck the underside of the crossbar, rebounded on to the back of the goalkeeper's neck, flattened him and ricocheted into the goal.

Barnsley, by virtue of Skinner's genius in scoring with the penalty and at the same time reducing the opponents to 10 men, won the game.

It was soon after, though, that Skinner for the first and last time met his match. Again it was a cup-tie and this time Barnsley were playing Arsenal at Highbury. Going down on the train with the crates of light ale under the seat, we agreed that if Skinner could frighten them Barnsley had a chance. But we didn't know that Arsenal had someone just as hard as Skinner and twice as clever. His name was Alec Forbes and Barnsley lost. Going sadly home, we agreed with the thought that if Barnsley had Forbes they'd soon get into the First Division. What we left unsaid was that they'd probably make it by default because other teams faced with the prospect of playing against a side containing both Skinner and Forbes would probably give Barnsley two points to stop at home.

Anyway things have changed now. Skinner has retired and there's no one to take his place. The last time I saw Barnsley in a cup-tie things were different. They played Manchester United at Barnsley and went down ever so politely 4–0. United played as if they had written the modern theory of the game and Barnsley as if they'd read it backwards. There were no fights either on or off the field, Denis Law shimmered like quicksilver and scored as he pleased, and a young lad called George Best played with the instinctive joy of a genius. There was only one flash of the old fighting spirit. As Law cheekily and magically dribbled round the wing half, stopped, showed him the ball, then beat him again, a bloke standing near us shouted, "Tha wouldn't have done that to Skinner, Denis." Those who remembered smiled. But knowingly.

From *Football Daft*, 1968

Flowers
Of Manchester

Anonymous

One cold and bitter Thursday in Munich, Germany,
Eight great football stalwarts conceded victory.
Eight men will never play again, who met destruction there
The Flowers of English football, the Flowers of Manchester.

Matt Busby's boys were flying returning from Belgrade,
This great united family all masters of their trade.
The pilot of the aircraft, the skipper Captain Thain,
Three times they tried to take off and twice turned back again.

The third time down the runway disaster followed close,
There was slush upon that runway and the aircraft never rose.
It ploughed into the marshy ground, it broke it overturned,
And eight of that team were killed when the blazing wreckage
   burned.

Roger Byrne and Tommy Taylor who were capped for England's
   side,
And Ireland's Billy Whelan and England's Geoff Bent died.
Mark Jones and Eddie Colman and David Pegg also,
They all lost their lives as it ploughed on through the snow.

Big Duncan he went too, with an injury to his brain,
And Ireland's brave Jack Blanchflower will never play again.
The great Matt Busby lay there, the father of this team,
Three long months passed by before he saw his team again.

The trainer, coach and secretary and a member of the crew,
Eight great sporting journalists who with United flew,
And one of them was Big Swifty who we will ne'er forget,
The finest English keeper that ever graced a net.

Oh England's finest football team it's record truly great,
It's proud successes mocked by a cruel turn of fate,
Eight men will never play again who met destruction there,
The Flowers of English Football, the Flowers of Manchester.

As recorded by *The Spinners*

A Load Of Old Analysis

Willis Hall

For some extraordinary and, to me at least, totally inexplicable reason, not a single sports editor invited me to represent him in the press box at Frankfurt's football stadium for Scotland's crunch match with Yugoslavia, in June, 1974. I decided, therefore, that if I couldn't be at the actual game, I would do the next best thing and watch it in surroundings where the tension would be rare, the conversation informed and intelligent, and the company impeccable. In short, I chose to spend that particular afternoon in a TV studio with a bunch of TV's soccer panelists.

ITV or BBC, I had asked myself. And after much thought, I settled for joining Brian Moore and his bunch of trendies, rather than sitting in with Jimmy Hill and his more sober-suited chappies. The final decision was made, I might add, not because I fancied the sartorial elegance of the commercial lot's tartan jackets, but rather because I shuddered at the thought of getting within the firing line of a bad joke from Lawrie McMenemy.

Having made my choice, a quick phone call and the matter was settled. I have friends in high places. The Head of Sport for London Weekend Television said that he would be delighted to have me in his studio, provided I behaved myself, remained shtum, and kept well out of the way of his perambulating cameras – which is why you didn't spot me on the telly, rubbing shoulders with the mighty.

All the same, I enjoyed myself immensely.

To refresh your memory, the soccer experts I met up with on that ITV panel, tartan jackets and all, were those engaging highland laddies: Bobby Moncur, Paddy Crerand, Derek McDougan, Malcolm McAllison, and Big Brian (Jock) Moore. Your actual Laird of London Weekend himself, Brian McCloughie, had been given the day off and was reported to be at his wee hoose the noo' in McBrighton, munching a haggis butty.

I spent the first part of the afternoon in idyllic surroundings, watching two race meetings at once on a battery of television screens in the World Cup Office. Not only that, but I also had the good sense to put my money on Caius, a 5–2 winner, and Assett, which romped home at 5–1 – the shrewdness of my racing judgement being unimpaired by the fact that Paddy Crerand was singing: "Six foot two, eyes of blue, Big Jim Holton's after you . . ." in the background.

"Do you often back winners?" asked a puzzled sports producer, as though mentally earmarking me for a post as a new TV tipster. "Not often, no," I admitted truthfully. The sports producer sighed, went about his sports producing business, and John Rickman lived to tip another day.

All the same, by three o'clock, which was the time we were due to go down to the World Cup studio, I was thirteen pound 50 in front, having also picked up place money on a well-priced outsider.

The panel, meanwhile, had gone through a sort of preliminary rough-and-ready rehearsal, more for the benefit of the studio technicians, it seemed, than to give the lads a chance to sharpen up their epigrams and witticisms. As I took my seat, a tasty make-up lady was dabbing powder at Brian Moore's receding hairline.

"Fifteen seconds, studio!" boomed a disembodied voice. And then we were transmitting. Dutifully, as ordered, I remained totally shtum and hid myself away from the prowling TV cameras.

I was not the only interloper in the studio. Clydesider, Jim Reid, was down in London and had free-loaded in on Paddy Crerand's invitation.

The panel's pre-match chat on Scotland's chances that afternoon was informed, albeit cautious:

"They *might* do it," said Malcolm Allison.

"They're in with a *chance*," opined Bobby Moncur.

"It could be a *draw*," mused Derek Dougan.

"I fancy them a *little* bit," observed Paddy Crerand, thoughtfully.

At Brian Moore's prompting they expanded further, still slightly dubious, as to *how* they thought that Scotland might snatch at opportunities. It was Allison's opinion that the Scots might catch the Yugoslavs ball-watching. Dougan said that the Yugoslavs were open to be exploited from corners. Crerand reckoned that Bremner and his lads could achieve the impossible by concentrating their attack on the left-hand side of the Yugoslav defence. The mood was changing from one of doubt to that of cautious optimism.

There was talk too, at length, of how it was neither good nor right nor fair to players to uproot them from their wives and families and lock them away in a hotel for four weeks. Which was strange, coming from a panel of men who had themselves been uprooted from their wives and families and settled in a hotel near the studio for the duration of the competition. Particularly as one of them had told me not half an hour before, that he was "having the time of his life, breakfast in bed, watching football all day long and getting paid for it."

Pause for commercial break, after which we were no longer transmitting from the studio, but receiving pictures and commentary direct from Frankfurt.

We all relaxed.

"Can somebody get Jimmy Reid a cup of tea?" asked Paddy Crerand, solicitously. Two studio men, both obviously fully paid-up Union members, rushed to oblige.

"Right, lads, jackets off," said Brian Moore. And off came all the tartan coats and even Jimmy Reid rolled his sleeves up. I settled myself happily in my chair and prepared to drink in the informed comments and intelligent analysis that lay in store for me from the mouths of my professional footballing companions.

On the screen, almost immediately after the kick-off, a Scottish pass went dangerously astray.

"Oh shit," said Derek Dougan, thus setting the level of comment for the afternoon.

"Go *on*, Sandy, go *on*, Sandy!" screamed Paddy Crerand.

"Get into him, Joe! *Kill* him, Joe!" exhorted someone of Jim Holton.

"Far post – it's a far post ball!" from Malcolm Allison.

Oh, come *on*, Billy, oh, come *on*, Billy!" groaned Paddy Crerand, who is blessed with the gift of poetic repetition.

"Diabolical that! Di-a-bloody-bolical!" and "Penalty, you bugger!" someone shouted at the game's arbiter.

"Who is this bloody referee?" asked someone else.

"He's a Mexican," said Brian Moore.

"He's a bloody Mexican bandit," said another.

" 'E's a quick bugger, int 'e, Oblak?" observed Malcolm Allison, thoughtfully.

"Oh shit," said Derek Dougan, as danger again threatened. Paddy Crerand, in his excitement, was bobbing up and down like a schoolboy impatient for the lavatory.

The first half of the game sped away like nobody's business. The dialogue in the studio may not have been informed, it may not have been intelligent, but it had been enthralling and totally engrossing.

"Jackets on, lads," said Brian Moore, about a minute before the end of the first half. The panelists donned their tartan coats and the make-up lady rushed forward to dab again at Brian Moore's shining and perspiring forehead. "As soon as we've taken the commercial break," he said, "I'll come to you again for quick one-line reactions."

Which seemed odd, because I thought he'd been hearing quick one-line reactions for forty-five minutes.

Fag-ends, cigar-butts, plastic tea-cups, a Clydeside Union man and a buckshee sportswriter all disappeared like magic – the studio was back on transmission during the game's interval.

"So far so good," murmured Brian Moore to the nation, and then invited his colleagues' comments. I held my breath and waited for the common language of the terraces to hit the ether.

"What a performance," said Derek Dougan, soberly.

"They're sure to win," murmured a suave Malcolm Allison, of Scotland's chances.

"The Yugoslavs must be little worried," was the urbane opinion of a collected Paddy Crerand.

"Scotland are the best side," analysed a cool, calm Bobby Moncur. "They're sure to win if they keep pegging away without getting too excited."

Without getting too excited? Precisely. All they had to do, it seemed, was behave exactly as the lads in the studio were doing. And as soon as the second half was under way, and the studio microphones were once more out of action, the analysts were at it again.

"Oh shit," said Derek Dougan, getting the ball immediately rolling. He repeated those exact words twice more during the second half: once when the news was flashed on the monitor that Brazil were leading Zaire by three goals to nil, and again when the Yugoslavs struck with their goal. Dougan's phrase, at that precise moment in time, seemed charged with majestic eloquence.

The panel's comments when the final whistle came were entirely unprintable. Their subsequent remarks to the cameras, when we were once again transmitting, were masterly understatements.

"What a shame," said Brian Moore.

"I'm disappointed. I'm very disappointed," said Paddy Crerand, his face as crumpled as last week's bed-linen.

Outside the studio, in the corridor, I met an elated producer. "You won't *believe* the shot we got of Paddy's face when the Yugoslavs scored," he said. "Tragic. A tragic shattered Scots supporter." I told him that I did believe him.

I also told him that, despite the result, I had enjoyed my afternoon immensely, and could I come back and do it again sometime, perhaps on the afternoon of the World Cup Final? He said probably, but it would depend upon the content of the article I wrote about his programme. Well, this was it. He also entertained me in his Hospitality Room, hospitably, at the end of the afternoon's transmission. It was then that my own reaction to the dismal result set in, and I went on drinking.

It was after one o'clock in the morning when I poured Jim Reid into a taxi. He was going, for some reason that still eludes me, to East Sheen. He had been a Scottish supporter alone in London on Scotland's night of tragedy, and I had taken him out and wined him and dined him. At least I had done something. It did not occur to me, until much later, that Jim and I had spent about six hours in each other's company on that sad Saturday night, we had argued and we had chatted, but not once – never, in the whole course of the evening – did we mention football.

From *The Evening Standard*, 1974

West German Spirit Wins Cup

Geoffrey Green

West Germany 2   Netherlands 1

In a tough, brittle and brilliant battle in the Olympic Stadium here today where every blade of grass was contested and sternly controlled by Jack Taylor, the English referee, in which he "booked" three players and awarded two penalty kicks inside the first half hour, West Germany came back from a black opening to take the new World Cup trophy. One of those penalties went to the Netherlands in the first minute for a dazzling flash of play by Cruyff, who was hooked up by Vogts. Neeskens firmly punished the Germans from the spot. Whoever before had such a beginning to a summit meeting and who before had to recover from such a seeming disaster?

But the Germans, highly skilled fighters, did it in the end with Müller almost inevitably – snatching the winner three minutes before half-time after Breitner had first put the scores level, also from the penalty spot. The Dutch in the end perhaps were a bit unlucky yet it was a great final because both sides were prepared to take chances in a competition which as a whole may not have been as good as that in Mexico. The Germans probably are a better side now than in 1966, but as always their greatest asset has been their untameable spirit.

So history repeated itself. In 1954 West Germany, having lost a match earlier in the competition, beat the vaunted Hungarians at Berne after being two goals behind inside the opening 10 minutes. This time also they had lost an earlier match, to the East Germans, but again came through to victory. Once more, too, the side that scored first in a world climax had the prize snatched from them. Indeed of the seven finals since the war only Brazil in Mexico four years ago hit the jackpot first and pocketed their winnings.

At the end of course in a sea of waving German flags the 82,000 crowd was delirious with delight as the Dutchmen in this vast concourse turned their heads on the past. In the presence, too, of some 1,700 pressmen and 1,200 radio and television commentators the distinguished guests headed by Prince Bernhard, of the Netherlands, saw the end of the beginning. Germany thus became the fourth host nation to win the trophy and the Netherlands after their long slog from the foothills just failed to scale this Everest of the game.

Right from that opening minute forces were set in motion and so quickly did events fall at each end and in midfield that it was like trying to catch reality on the wing. On parade were the representatives of three of the great club sides in Europe – Bayern Munich – six of them in the German side – Ajax, of Amsterdam, and Feyenoord of Rotterdam. But for some great saves by Maier, under the German crossbar, over the last stages the Dutch indeed might have beaten off the shadow. But the goalkeeper is a part of the team and Maier played his part to the full.

In a drama designed to bring out the human factors, which were slowly unravelled, both sides all the way were twisting and turning to all points of the compass to outwit one another; the tackling also was uncompromising. Certainly the fat seemed to be in the fire for the Germans as the Netherlands football began to sizzle from the beginning after that vital penalty kick in the opening seconds. But Vogts the culprit of that moment in the end became one of Germany's heroes. He it was who was detailed to put Cruyff in fetters. He failed in that first minute but the longer the battle went the further he drove the brilliant Dutchman away from the danger spots in the German penalty area, and it was his battling performance that perhaps helped Germany to hang on as the scales tilted at the end.

For the opening seconds the Dutch caressed the ball crossfield at a walking pace as if trying to mesmerise the opposition. Suddenly like the Brazilians of old there was a flash of lightning from Cruyff, picking up the pass from Neeskens, he suddenly changed gear and pace and was through the German defence with the speed of a kingfisher. In desperation Vogts got him from behind and Neeskens did the rest from the spot.

After 25 minutes the German game was already on the mend, calmly directed by Beckenbauer from the back and carried on by the beautiful long passing of Overath to Müller and his wingers Grabowski and Holzenbein. It was one of these moves, in which Breitner was also concerned, that Holzenbein helped by Breitner's decoy move, cut in, was hooked up by Jansen and there next was Breitner to put Germany level from the penalty.

Seven minutes from the interval Cruyff with a sudden break from midfield teased Beckenbauer as the German captain tried to protect an open situation, deluded him, fed Neeskens on his own to the left only to see Maier make the first of his great saves point blank. Netherlands should have been ahead then, but instead three minutes from the interval it was Bonhof, breaking quickly down the right who squared the ball to see Müller on the half turn pick his spot inside the far post superbly and leap like a grasshopper to the skies in delight.

There the score remained to the end but not before Rijsbergen had once saved off his line from Holzenbein and Maier saved from Van Hanegem's diving header; from Neeskens and then from Neeskens again with only a quarter of an hour left – another blistering block this from a full volley. By half-time Vogts, Van Hanegem, Neeskens and Cruyff had all received the yellow card from Mr Taylor and there might have been another penalty. Still the battle was exciting enough without further missed heartbeats.

At the interval the Netherlands brought on Van de Kerkhof for Rensenbrink who, though having passed a fitness test in the morning, was clearly not 100 per cent. With 20 minutes left and the Netherlands making their final assault to save themselves, they brought on De Jong for the injured Rijsbergen. But in spite of a grandstand finish they just could not squeeze that last goal.

So a colourful scene ended as the pulses quickened. In the distance the Olympic tower was a thin pencil pointing to the clouds. Underneath the futuristic covering of the stadium – resembling a mosquito net – the gnats of fate stung. How many countless other millions watched it on television is anybody's guess.

Down on the field both sides had a whiff of vision, exemplified particularly by Beckenbauer and by Cruyff in spite of Vogts his jailer. There was no conventional expression. This was modern football to a high degree. The originality was unlaboured and amid it all there was Overath with his crisp, shrewd eye and his style for spotting a weakness. On either side, too, there was a certain innate swagger by Grabowski and Neeskens who must now feel that he might have scored three times but for Maier.

WEST GERMANY: J. Maier (1); H. Vogts (2), P. Breitner (3), H. Schwarzenbeck (4), F. Beckenbauer (5), R. Bonhof (16), U. Höness (14), J. Grabowski (9), W. Overath (12), G. Müller (13), B. Holzenbein (17).

NETHERLANDS: J. Jongbloed (8), W. Suurbier (20), A. Haan (2), W. Rijsbergen (17) (sub. T. de Jong (7)), R. Krol (12), W. Jansen (6), W. Van Hanegem (3), J. Neeskens (13), J. Rep (16), J. Cruyff (14), R. Rensenbrink (15) (sub. R. Van de Kerkhof (10)).

Referee: J. Taylor (England).

From *The Times*, 1974.

ACKNOWLEDGEMENTS

Acknowledgements and grateful thanks are due to the following authors and publishers for their kind permission to reproduce the contents of this book.

To J. B. Priestley and William Heinemann Ltd for the extract from *The Good Companions*

To Alan Simpson and Hampton Town Football Club for "Allez Hampton" and "Innovations"

To *Sportsworld* for "Child's Play" and "Bridging the Gap"

To Peter Terson and Penguin Books Ltd for the extract from *The Apprentices*

To Harold Pinter and Eyre Methuen Ltd for the extract from *The Dumb Waiter*

To Jack Rosenthal and the *Evening Standard* for "Cup Final, 2070"

To Julie Welch and *The Observer* for "Hard Man, Soft Centre"

To Derek Dougan and Allison & Busby Ltd for the extract from *The Sash He Never Wore*

To Michael Carey and *The Observer* for "Fizz it About"

To Brian Glanville and Martin Secker & Warburg Ltd for "The Dying Footballer" from *The Director's Wife and Other Stories* and also for the title story from *The Thing He Loves*

To Ian Wooldridge and the *Daily Mail* for "The Manager"

To Johnny Speight for "Bert Shakespeare: Fuhrer"

To The Spinners for "The Flowers of Manchester"

To Alan Sillitoe and W. H. Allen & Co Ltd for "The Match" from *The Loneliness of the Long Distance Runner*

To Derek Dougan and Pelham Books Ltd for the extract from *Derek Dougan's Book of Soccer No. 2*

To Richard Bates and *The Sunday Times* for "Amateur Cup Final, 1956" by H. E. Bates

To Hunter Davies and *The Sunday Times Magazine* for "Oh, No, Not Him Again!"

To Hunter Davies and *The Sunday Times* for "Liverpool Star"

To Tony Pawson and Eyre Methuen Ltd for the extract from *The Football Managers*

To Arthur Hopcraft and *The Observer* for "World Cup Championship, 1968"

To Leslie Vernon and *World Soccer* for "Scapegoats"

To Julie Welch, Peter Corrigan, Alan Road and *The Observer* for "Three Fives"
To Geoffrey Green and *The Times* for "Sweden v Brazil, 1958", "West Germany v England, 1970" and "Leeds v Sunderland, 1973"
To John Moynihan and *The Sunday Telegraph* for "Bad Guy turns Good Guy"
To Danny Blanchflower and *The Sunday Express* for "One More Time"
To Willis Hall and the *Evening Standard* for "A Load Of Old Analysis"
To Geoffrey Green and *The Times* for "West German Spirit Wins Cup"
To Arthur Hopcraft and William Heinemann Ltd for the extract from *The Great Apple Raid*
To Stanley Paul & Co Ltd for the extracts from *Football Daft*
And to Bill Tidy and *Punch* Publications Ltd for permission to reproduce all the cartoons contained in this book.